Where Have You Seen God?

—— *Recognizing the Divine Presence in Everyday Life* ——

BY Keva Green

FOREWORD BY
Alyce M. McKenzie

RESOURCE *Publications* · Eugene, Oregon

WHERE HAVE YOU SEEN GOD?
Recognizing the Divine Presence in Everyday Life

Resource Publications
An Imprint of Wipf and Stock Publishers
199 W. 8th Ave., Suite 3
Eugene, OR 97401

www.wipfandstock.com

PAPERBACK ISBN: 978-1-5326-9078-5
HARDCOVER ISBN: 978-1-5326-9079-2
EBOOK ISBN: 978-1-5326-9080-8

Scriptures taken from the Holy Bible, New International Version®, NIV®. Copyright © 1973, 1978, 1984, 2011 by Biblica, Inc.™ Used by permission of Zondervan. All rights reserved worldwide. www.zondervan.com The "NIV" and "New International Version" are trademarks registered in the United States Patent and Trademark Office by Biblica, Inc.™

Manufactured in the U.S.A.   09/12/19

To my precious family,
I definitely see God moving in and around you
LeeRand, Kevin, Liz, London, Rain, and Boston.

Where Have You Seen God?

Feb. 2020

Dear Jared,

Thank you for making
this a reality. May you
recognize God moving all
around you.

Love,
Keva

Contents

Foreword by Alyce M. McKenzie | xi

Acknowledgments | xiii

The Beginning of the Journey

1   Seeing God | 3

2   A Deal with God | 7

3   With God's Help | 14

4   Kissing Toes | 17

5   Talking to God | 20

6   You Have to Look Up to See Rainbows | 22

7   Obeying the Whisper | 26

8   Falling Star | 30

Seminary Life

9   Sharing a Part of Me | 39

10   Carried by God | 46

11   An Angel's View | 50

12   God Provides | 54

13   Holy Appetizer | 58

14   The Power of Hospitality | 61

15   God Know Our Needs | 64

16   Seeing the Face of God | 66

17   Why Me, Lord? | 71

18   It Is Not about Me | 75

Life in England

19   Clerical Trousers | 85

20   Blessings within Disappointments | 87

21   A New Prayer Ministry | 91

22   Amazing Grace | 93

23   When God Shakes Our World | 95

24   The Gate Is Narrow | 98

25   Thinking They Know | 100

26   A Different Perspective | 102

27   Daring to Touch | 108

28   An Opportunity to Preach | 112

Back in Texas

29   A Precious Gift | 119

30   The Number of Hairs on Your Head | 122

31   Being a Life Caddy | 124

32   Hearing God's Voice | 126

33   Strangely Warmed | 130

34   Praying for Rain | 134

35   God's Will and God's Timing | 139

36   Prayer Partners | 144

37   Sometimes You Just Have to Dance | 146

Experiences Around the World

38   An Icy Volcano | 151

39   From Killing Fields to New Life | 155

40   Baptizing in India | 160

41   New Eyes to See God | 164

42   God Knows the Depth | 166

43   God Speaks All Languages | 169

44   Walk a Mile in My Shoes | 172

Looking Ahead

45 Faith Pointing | 181

46 Epilogue: In Your Life . . . Where Have You Seen God? | 185

Supported Ministries/Charities | 189

Foreword

by Alyce M. McKenzie

I FIRST MET KEVA Green several years ago when she was a student in my Introduction to Preaching class at Perkins School of Theology. I came to appreciate her work ethic, her careful preparation, and her creativity. But what struck me most about her was her luminous joy. In her sermons preached in class she shared the faith that had come through her struggles, the obstacles and setbacks she had encountered in life.

In *Where Have You Seen God?* Keva shares turning points in her faith journey as teaching moments both for herself and readers. The book unfolds as a series of "divine encounters" from her young adulthood, seminary years, ministry in England, and life in Texas since her return. Like life itself, they cover a spectrum of moods and emotions: poignant, humorous, and joyful. They range from God seeing her through the death of her mother, to the love she observes between a long-married couple, to a rainbow at a funeral, to a homeless man reading the Bible on a curb, to the moon glowing through parted clouds. These are just a few of the relatable moments that will inspire readers to learn valuable life lessons such as dealing with disappointment, appreciating daily blessings, and discerning divine guidance for the path ahead. These divine encounters range around the world, from her own and others' experiences in Texas, England, Cambodia, India, and Spain.

Where Have You Seen God? depicts God as transcendent creator, but also as intimate revealer in the mundane details and experiences of daily life. For Keva, God is ever present, right alongside us in our life journey. God's presence is more than enough to calm our fears and infuse us with courage.

In my own work on creativity and preaching, I call for us to cultivate a "knack for noticing," attentiveness to where God is seeking to communicate with us through our inner and outer lives. Keva's "divine encounters" are the fruits of her attentiveness. They comfort us with a depiction of God as the constant initiator of contact with us. They challenge us to do our part in the relationship by noticing and responding to God's invitations with faith and courage. *Where Have You Seen God?* serves as a tutorial in discernment, staying attentive to one's own inner life and to one's experiences in the world, and, with God's help, making sense of the unfolding story of each of our lives. It models hyper attentiveness to God's presence for readers to emulate. It invites readers to join the journey and to record our own stories for our family, friends, and the wider world.

In the epilogue, Keva offers practical guidance on how we can share our own stories and informs us that the proceeds from sales of the book will go toward several causes she supports: Children's Organ Transplant Association, Heart for Cambodia, My Father's House Orphanage in India, and High Rise Day Habilitation Center. She reminds us we have been "blessed to be a blessing," and invites us to support these and other causes to improve our world.

She ends on a hopeful, but challenging note: "God is moving in so many mighty ways around us. Let's not miss an opportunity to be a part of it. I hope this book has opened your eyes to some of the ways that you can be aware of God's presence. My greatest prayer for you is that you will recognize the divine presence of God all around you every single day! Amen and amen!"

Acknowledgments

I HAVE BEEN BLESSED by seeing God move in so many wonderful ways throughout my lifetime. Of course, the greatest blessings have been all of the amazing individuals who have touched my life. This book is made up of many of those stories where God brought us together and allowed us to experience the fullness of God's glory in a variety of ways.

I am humbled by all those who have played a part in this book, either through sharing their story or in helping me to write and publish this manuscript. First and foremost, thank you so very much to my dear family who have loved me and supported me throughout the years. Thanks to my wonderful parents, Lee and "Tooter" Harrison, who taught me about God from an early age and then demonstrated what it looked like to live a life of faith. I miss the two of you and look forward to when we meet again in heaven.

LeeRand and Kevin, my precious children, I am so incredibly blessed to have you. I am so very proud of both of you and how God has used you in so many ways. Thanks for always making everything an adventure and so much fun. A special thanks to my beautiful daughter-in-law, Liz, who is not only a special part of the family but is also an important part of my marketing and publicity team. Also, thanks to Kevin and Liz for their greatest achievements in giving me three perfect grandchildren: London, Rain, and Boston.

Mark Harrison is the best big brother a girl could have. Thank you for being there for me throughout the years. Thanks to my sister-in-law, Linda, for your support. And a special thanks to my nephew Gray and his family, Maddie, Keegan, and Audrey, for allowing me to share your powerful story. Your family continues to be a witness to so many people and a powerful support for children with fragile medical needs.

When I look back through the years, I realize how God has touched my life with so many wonderful family members. A few are mentioned in the book, but all have had a major impact on my life. I thank God for Judy,

Michael, Randolph and Evelyn, Gene and Virgie, Becca, Helene, Marilois, and too many others to try to name. Love to each of you.

Thank goodness for girlfriends! Since my earliest memories I have had a group of close friends who have made life exciting. They were the ones with whom I could share my secrets and my dreams. We would laugh together and cry together. And what a blessing that for the majority of these dear friends, we could pray together and grow in faith together. Some of these sweet friends were also part of my "quads" in the various places I have lived, and we made it a point to get together on a regular basis to talk about where we had seen God. Each of them plays an important part of this book. Thanks and love to: Barbara, Susan, Mary, Ginger, Sheri, Patricia, Pat, Barbara, Jan, Holly, Carol, Chris, Anne, Liz, Patty, Edith, Shirley, Janet, Pat, Annie, Norma, Marian, Sharmy, Deb, Cindy, Rebecca, Lindy, Sue, Shannon, Deborah, Judy, Connie, Jan, Cindy, Mary, Nancy, Jennifer, Phyllis, Cathy, Janine, Mary, Amanda, and so many others.

There are many of my seminary and clergy friends who are included in some of these stories. Thanks to those who allowed me to share where I saw God in your life and thanks to all of you for making a difference in my life: Dr. William J. Abraham, Rev. Godfrey Hubert, Tracy Anne Allred, Dr. Alyce McKenzie, Dr. Stan Copeland, David McLarin, Dr. Dudley Dancer, Dr. Tom Hudspeth, Rev. Donna Whitehead, Rev. Mike Tyson, Dr. William S. Babcock, Bishop Scott Jones, Dr. Roy Heller, Rev. Bill Bryan, Rev. Liz Talbert, Rev. Bob Johnson, Father Darryl Jordan, Rev. Sean Adair, Rev. Alistair Sharp, Rev. Vernon Marsh, Dr. Richard Dunagin, and Rev. Chiv In. Serving in ministry can sometimes be a challenge and so I feel incredibly blessed to have walked beside these and so many other faithful servants of the Lord.

Of course, a special thank you to the congregations I have served and the many churches where I have had the privilege to preach. You have all taught me more about what it means to walk in faith. A heartfelt thanks to those congregations who have supported and encouraged me to share God's Word whether from the pulpit or in my writing.

There are so many individuals and couples from the various churches who have been particularly supportive. Some are mentioned in the Divine Encounters throughout the book. There are also those who supported the writing of this book by providing me a lake house or caravan on the cliffs or opened their homes to me so that I could slip away and focus on writing. There are those who read the manuscript and gave suggestions. And there are those who just continually encouraged me and pushed me to put these stories on paper so that others could read them. To all of you I give my sincere thanks that God put you in my life: Norma, Joel and Barbara, Raymond, Frank, Linda, Sean and Alison, Jonathan, Dave and Anne, Walter and Mary, Les and Betty, Keith and Rita, Phil, Harry and Kathleen, Bill and Ann, Greg and Sandy, Dan and Carol, Scott and Sue, Luke and Kas, Darren and Anne, Elke, Carol, Agustin, Faith and Marti, Jeri, Jessica, Nancy and David, J. W. and Cathy, and many other longtime and newfound friends in America and throughout the world.

A special thanks to consultants Lynn Kitchens and Jared Rosen with DreamSculpt for all of your assistance. Thanks also to my publisher and those who have been so supportive at Wipf and Stock. I appreciate your guiding me through the process, particularly Matt Wimer and Daniel Lanning.

Most of all, I am incredibly humbled by the multitude of blessings that God has given me, and the many ways the Lord's love has been demonstrated to me. Lord, you are my God and I pray that as I share these Divine Encounters that others' eyes might be opened to you so that they too might experience who you truly are. May everything I do glorify your Name. Amen.

The Beginning of the Journey

Seeing God

THIS IS A BOOK of stories—stories about God and stories about how God miraculously appears to us even in our daily lives. I am always amazed that the Lord God Almighty loves us enough to be intimately involved in our lives. The beginning of the Gospel of Matthew talks about the birth of Jesus and in the prophecy of his birth it is said that he will be called Immanuel—meaning "God with us."[1] That is why he came into this world—to be with us. At the end of the Gospel of Matthew, Jesus is giving his final message to his disciples with these words: "And surely I am with you always, to the very end of the age."[2]

Does anyone else find that incredible? I love the knowledge that God is with me at all times and in all places. There is nowhere that we can go that God is not with us. As David said so poetically in Psalm 139:

> [7] Where can I go from your Spirit?
>
> Where can I flee from your presence?
>
> [8] If I go up to the heavens, you are there;
>
> if I make my bed in the depths, you are there.
>
> [9] If I rise on the wings of the dawn,
>
> if I settle on the far side of the sea,
>
> [10] even there your hand will guide me,
>
> your right hand will hold me fast.

And as Paul so eloquently stated in Romans 8—there is absolutely nothing that can separate us from the love of God.

> [38] For I am convinced that neither death nor life, neither angels nor demons, neither the present nor the future, nor any powers,

1. Matt 1:23.
2. Matt 28:20.

[39] neither height nor depth, nor anything in all creation, will be able to separate us from the love of God that is in Christ Jesus our Lord.

I remember a dear Christian friend telling me one time that he thought God created the earth and then just stepped away from creation. He clearly had whole-hearted belief in the existence of God, but he did not think the Lord Almighty Creator of the Universe bothered with the miniscule things in our daily lives. He figured God was too big to be involved with us mere humans. I was shocked by my friend's view and quickly explained that it was because I truly believed God was an incredibly big God that I figured the Divine could not only handle the things of heaven, but also be intimately and actively involved in our lives. After all, Psalm 139:2–4 talks about God knowing when we sit and when we rise and perceiving our thoughts from afar and even knowing our words before they are on our tongue. I figure that is a pretty intimate God who is truly "with us."

Knowing that God is with me impacts my life in powerful ways. Of course, there are those times when I get wrapped up in my own affairs and I forget that God is with me, like the times when I get so busy checking things off my ministry to-do list and start thinking I am doing it out of my own strength and for my own benefit. Those are usually the times when I do selfish, inappropriate things. Yet it is glorious when I am fully focused on the fact that God is with me. Those seem to be the times when I am more aware and sensitive to the sacred nature of life all around me and God's divine fingerprints showing up in marvelous ways.

Over twenty years ago I was blessed to be a part of a small group of women from our church at Foundry United Methodist in Houston. We would get together once a week for an hour, and we would share life and share God. There were certain questions that we would ask each other each week in order to hold us all accountable in our faith. The first one was: "Where have you seen God?" This was such a powerful question for me because it taught me to start paying attention to how God is moving all around me every single day. I had always known that God was actively involved in my life, but I usually got so busy with things that I would forget to pay attention to the Lord's divine presence in my day-to-day life. Yet since I knew that each week I would be meeting with these special friends, it made me more sensitive and aware of the God-things so that I was prepared to share them.

The other powerful question that we would discuss at the end of our time was to go around and ask, "Where do you need God?" We would then share our prayer requests so that we could continually lift each other up to the Lord throughout the week. Maybe we were aware of a medical test coming up or a strenuous situation that we were dealing with at work or a family concern. Whatever the issue was with which we were struggling, we could share it in this safe environment and state that we knew we needed God's presence and guidance and handling. It was a prayer request that we knew the others would take seriously and would continually lift to the Lord.

The question "Where have you seen God?" has continued to be a powerful influence in my life. It is a question that a group of my seminary friends would ask each other when we happened to pass on campus. It was a way of encouraging each other and keeping our focus on the Lord.

Then when I served for a few years in England as a pastor, I asked my clergy friends and the various churches that question and have always been inspired by their answers. And it is certainly a question I continue to ask since I have moved back to Texas.

One of my good friends, Norma Stachura, and I try to get together at least once a month, and it is a special time to share Mexican food and all of our God-sightings since the last time we have been together. It is so much fun for me to keep track of all the different instances of what God is doing so that when we have our time together, I can share each one with her. And it is amazing to hear all of her stories of how God's holy presence has affected her life and the astonishing places that she has seen God moving all around her. Is there someone in your life with whom you can make it a point to share those God moments that you are experiencing? Someone with whom you can trust and enjoy sharing such sacred revelations?

Ever since that first small group of women back in Houston that had such a powerful impact on my life, I have tried to make sure that I pull together three or four women in each ministry setting so that we could meet weekly and share God experiences. I believe that God is always with us, but I also believe that one of the great supports in the Christian life is to have a close connection with others who are strong in faith so that we can share life. And in all of those groups as we have gathered through the years our main question to ask is: "Where have you seen God?"

There is absolutely no way that I can document all of the God experiences by which I have been blessed, but I at least wanted to put down in writing some of the major ones. The stories in this book include those major turning points in my life where it was obvious that God was directing my steps. It also includes some of the teaching moments where God opened my eyes to what is important. These stories are distilled from my own personal God-experiences, as well as observing God's presence in the life of my family and close friends. It has been amazing to watch God move in such magnificent ways in their lives. And I feel privileged to share some of their inspiring God-sightings. All of these stories have been shared at different times, either in preaching and speaking opportunities, or while visiting with friends. After sharing the stories, I would often have someone request a written copy of them. Various individuals encouraged me to write these down so that others could be encouraged in their faith. So, this book is my attempt to at least capture some of these wonderful God moments.

What I have come to realize through the years is God is always around us and active in our lives. Yet often we are so busy with the things of this world we miss out on fully recognizing what God is doing and experiencing all the divine events happening in our daily activities. I am no more important to God than you are; I have just learned to keep my eyes open so that I am getting better at recognizing what God is doing on a daily basis. I know for some people that they only recognize that it is God when it is an earth-shattering, life-changing, miraculous moment. God is certainly in those moments as well, but unfortunately most people miss the small little divine whispers that are also heart-warming encouragements. After all, sometimes it is the little things that happen where you see the twinkle in an eye and you feel the prod of God saying, "Did you catch that? That was a love nudge from me!"

I am hoping as you read these stories, they will awaken something deep inside of you so you experience God's divine nature in your everyday life. Use the questions after each story to ponder those experiences that you have already had or to open your eyes for future revelations. Life is so very precious and there are so many layers of life that are full of deeper understandings and significance. Often people only skim the top layer and miss the intricate beauty that is connected to all of our experiences. I encourage you to fully breathe in every moment and every level of where God is working in your life. My prayer is that these stories will be a blessing to you and an encouragement for you to keep your eyes open for where you see God.

A Deal with God

THERE ARE SOME THINGS that you just accept as true—without any doubt. I guess for me that was how I felt about the existence of God. It was one of those things that I learned at an early age and then never questioned. Sort of like the concept of breathing air that we can't see, I knew that God existed even if I could not see the Lord's presence right in front of me. And of course, if God exists then you should be able to talk. So even as a little girl I would talk to God—guess you could say the proper word was 'pray', but sometimes that seemed too formal of a term. So, when my wonderful Christian parents taught me that there was a God who knew everything about me and heard me when I talked, then I believed it. I learned from a very early age just to carry on conversations with God and to talk to the Divine about my feelings and my perceptions of life, just like you would talk with a close friend.

Of course, some things are so familiar to us that we end up taking them for granted and maybe that was what happened to my relationship with the Lord. When I was young, I was very involved in church and youth group activities, but later when I went off to the university, I sort of pushed my relationship with God to the back burner. I still knew God existed and knew if I needed, I could pray and talk to the Lord. But unfortunately, it was a time in my life when I was much more into me and what I wanted, and knowing God seemed less important.

While at Texas A&M University, I met a wonderful young man and fell madly in love with him. He was gentle and loving and very handsome! We could talk about anything under the sun or just sit and stare into each other's eyes. We decided we wanted to marry, and the only concern was that he was from a strong Catholic family and I was from a strong Baptist one. Actually, that was not a problem for us since we figured we both worshipped the same God, just in a little different fashion. So, we married and decided that we would compromise by joining a church that fell somewhere in the middle of the Catholic/Baptist spectrum. We visited the United Methodist Church and felt it was a good middle ground, and so as a young married couple we began going there. It was a church that had just the right amount of liturgy so that you felt there was a strong foundation of belief and at the same time the preaching was biblically based. We enjoyed the praise and worship, and the congregation made us feel incredibly welcome. Unfortunately, that particular church had some issues come up with the minister and some of the members. To be honest, since we were new to the church we never really understood what the inner conflict was, but we did watch as it seemed to split the church in three ways: a third went with the minister to be part of another denomination, a third of the congregation remained United Methodist and stayed with the church building, and about a third went out the door. We were in the last third. All this mess was a little too weird for us, and so it gave us a great excuse just to stay away for a while.

During that time, we were both busy with our careers and had two small children, and so weekends became times when we were busy with other activities—riding bikes, going to the lake, running in races, going camping. Of course, we had kept our membership at the church, but you might say that we had subscribed to the "holiday plan"—we would only go at Christmas and Easter.

We lived in Houston at the time, and my parents, who lived in West Texas, would come to see us every once in a while. They would always encourage us to get involved in church. I remember my mother telling me that it was important that we were actively involved in church for our marriage and for our children and just for how we were living our lives. I let her know that I was handling my life just fine, thank you very much, and I did not need God, but if I did, I certainly knew where to find him.

One beautiful spring day in 1995, everything changed. All of a sudden, I was overwhelmed with devastating news. The FBI building in Oklahoma City had been bombed, and closer to home, my mother had just been diagnosed with colon cancer. I was crushed by how quickly life can take a drastic turn and how helpless you can feel during a crisis. My mother had always been someone to admire. She was the type of woman that when she walked into a room, you knew she was there by her presence and her grace. She was tall and beautiful with dark hair and dark eyes and a loving smile. And to me, she was my strength and my advisor and the one that I could lean on. I guess I never imagined that she could get sick or something might happen to her. I was shocked and hurting and scared.

It is amazing how when there is a crisis in our lives we can instantly come back to God, even if right before, when things were going great, we thought we could handle it all on our own. When I came running back, it was full force. I became more involved with my faith in multiple areas. I joined a

Sunday School class and a Disciple Bible Study group. I became a lay leader and volunteered for various roles in the church, and even joined the choir (which if you could hear me sing, you would find this very surprising). Somehow in my mind I had convinced myself that my mother had cancer because I had not been faithful in my walk as a Christian and had not been involved in church. I was determined to live a perfect life so God would heal my mom. I had this idea that if there was some way I could do absolutely everything to perfection and never make a single mistake, that maybe my reward would be that God would make my mother well. (By the way, this is not good theology, but it was what I was thinking at the time.)

That was the beginning of my trying to make deals with God. Have you ever tried to make deals with God? You know, those types of negotiations (or attempted manipulations) where you say, "Lord, if you will do this thing that I really want, then I promise I will do such-and-such."

My deals started with my going back to church but extended to all areas of my life—work habits, eating, exercising, everything. I had been a runner for a while and would normally get up early in the morning and go running before getting ready for work. Now I was getting up an hour earlier and doing my Bible study and then going out and running in the dark, praying for my mom. I would make more deals as I ran: "Lord, I'll run this next mile in eight minutes if you will heal my mom" or "I'll run fourteen miles today, Lord, if you'll heal my mom." (I know this really seems strange to be trying to make deals like this, but somehow at the time it seemed to make sense to me.) My most impressive deal was to attempt to run a marathon on my fortieth birthday (which was coming up the next spring) and to do it to honor my mother in hopes that God would heal her. I knew it would take a lot of training and getting prepared, but that would be my offering to God in hopes that he would in return make her well.

Now of course this "deal with God" was not something that I could share with my family. I just told them that I wanted to run the marathon on my birthday in honor of my mother (after all, she was there when I had been born those many years before). My mom seemed to think it was a neat idea I was doing it for her and would often refer to it as "her" marathon. Every day when I would run, I would talk to God about "our deal" of my running the marathon and that the Lord's part was to heal Mom. And—this is the cool part—I knew it must be a God-thing because when I looked to see if there was a marathon on my birthday that year . . . the only one on the list was in Maui!!! It must be a God-thing! The Lord wanted to send me to Hawaii to run this marathon for "our deal."

In the time leading up to the marathon, I would talk to my mom on the phone fairly often to check on how she was doing. One day a couple months before the marathon we were visiting, and she said that she had been to the doctor that day. She made the comment that she told him he needed to keep her alive until after "her big marathon." I was so shocked by her comment. I told her, "Mom, you are going to be just fine. God is going to heal you." I knew I could not tell her about the deal I had made with God, but in my mind, I was thinking how surprised and delighted she would be after I ran the marathon and then she immediately started getting well.

The time came for the race and my husband and I headed for Maui. It was fabulous. The lush beauty of Hawaii was beyond what I had expected. I had seen pictures but realized that being there in person was so much more of a feast to the senses. And I know part of my ecstatic delight to be there was that for months I had excitedly anticipated coming to this scenic place to finish my portion of our deal because I believed God, who is always faithful, would do what we had discussed. I absolutely knew without a doubt—my mom's health would radically improve.

Maui is one of those places where everywhere you look takes your breath away. It seemed like the colors were on high intensity with the blues of the ocean and the sky being more vivid than ever imagined and the greens of all the plants seeming to jump out at you, along with the indescribable variety of flora that accented every view. And the shape of land underneath that lush vegetation was also fascinating with the irregular-shaped mountains and cliffs, as well as edged with stunning beaches. It felt like a rare privilege to be able to run a marathon in such a place where you were so energized by all of God's creation that was around you.

The marathon began before sunrise on one side of the island in Kahului, and the road took us past Haleakalā Volcano just as the spectacular sunrise was painting the sky behind it. My sweet husband ran the first part of the marathon with me to keep me company, but since he had not trained for the entire 26.2 miles, he stopped about midway because he did not want to slow me down. He said he would catch a ride the rest of the way and be at the finish line when I got there to celebrate. He knew how much this marathon meant to me, since it was in honor of my dear mother. He wanted the marathon to be a perfect culmination to my months of intense preparing and focus.

The remainder of the marathon route was along the majestic cliffs looking over the sparkling ocean. You could see boats in the distance and hear the whales singing. We passed through the picturesque fishing village of Lahaina and then on a couple of miles farther to a flower-covered finish line in Kaanapali. It was such a powerful experience to be running this particular race. I had run other marathons in the past, but none of them had the significance this one did or were in such scenic locations. In prior races there was always a point where exhaustion would be overwhelming, and I would hit "the wall" a few miles from the end. Runners often start walking or just stop completely thinking they cannot go another step. Yet for this race it seemed like I was more energized, excited, and empowered with each step as I got closer and closer to the finish line. I had my mom's name written on my number, and there seemed to be a supernatural power supporting me every step of the way. I just knew as I came nearer to the finish line that God was healing my mother and making her well.

The race director knew it was my fortieth birthday and that I was running the marathon in honor of my mother, so he met me at the finish line with a flower lei to place around my neck. There was both an excitement of completing something special, and the thrill that even better things were ahead.

My husband and I celebrated after the race and then called home to let my mom know I had finished "her" race. But Dad answered the phone and said it was time to come home. I started explaining we were going to stay for the week and see all of the sights. But he just said again it was time to come home—now.

We started making rush plans trying to figure out how to get back to Texas. I ended up flying to Dallas, where my brother picked me up. We started driving out to West Texas before it was too late. My husband flew on to Houston to get the children and then make the long drive. When my brother and I arrived at my parents' home it was the middle of the night. Mom was already in a coma. This was not the way this was supposed to end. I'd finished the race! I'd given it all I had. I could not comprehend what I had done wrong. I thought it had been enough to save her. In the stillness of the early morning I knew I could not hang on to her any longer. I had the chance to kneel beside her and let her know I had finished "her" race and she could let go now. She passed away within two hours of our getting home.

Mom really had hung on long enough until I finished the race. She knew all along that her cancer was terminal. I think everyone else realized it too. Yet I had been so blind. I never once considered she would die . . . after all, I had a deal with God! This was so incredibly difficult because not only had I lost my mother and best friend, but I had lost my God—the one I always knew I could count on; the one who was supposed to always be there for me and hear my prayers and answer them.

The next few months my life seemed to fall apart. I could not function as a wife or a mother. I managed a large organization at work and could not keep my mind on what I needed to be doing. I was so emotional about everything and was constantly crying over the smallest of things. My sweet husband and children tried to support me. I was not coping well. And then our church announced that it was going to offer a Bible Study called *Experiencing God*. It was one my parents had taken a couple of years before. I remembered how they talked about it being life changing. I was still trying to figure out this

God, who I once thought I knew, so I decided maybe it would help to take the course. I started it while continuing my morning routine of getting up early to do my Bible study and then running each day.

One evening was particularly difficult for me. I could not stop crying. It seemed like my whole world was crumbling around me. I was overwhelmed with depression and grief. Everything I had attempted to do lately seemed like it was a disaster. On this night the darkness and pain seemed to be at such intensity that all hope was gone. I could not get control of my emotions. I stayed awake the entire night. I was not able to calm my emotions. When the alarm went off at the usual early time, I decided instead of sitting down to do my Bible study, I would go running. I got out in the dark and ran as hard as I could. I cursed God for not being there for me, for not doing what I thought the Lord God Almighty was supposed to do. "After all, God, I did my part of the bargain. I tried to be perfect. I went to church. I studied the Bible. Everything in life that I did—I tried to do it just right. I trained for months and all those hours of running I would talk to you about my mom and we agreed you would heal her. We talked about it. We talked about it!!!" And then all of a sudden I realized, *we* did not talk about it. *I* talked about it. And then I started thinking, "God, you allowed me to talk about it. You listened to me and let me go for months thinking we had a deal, and you never stopped me. God, we think that you talk to us, but you don't. We think you are speaking to us, but it is just us fooling ourselves while you sit there and watch. You don't really speak to us, do you?"

I came back home. I was furious with this latest realization of God. I felt betrayed by the Lord. I knew without a doubt God existed, but now I was beginning to think that God was just cruel for allowing us to convince ourselves of heavenly love and divine intervention, when instead the Lord just sits back and watches without saying a word. I came in the house; walked past the table where my Bible and *Experiencing God* workbook were sitting; and thought to myself I will never pick up the Bible again or have anything to do with God. That was it—relationship over!

Then I thought I would give God just one more chance. I would do one more lesson just to see if God had anything to say and if not, then that was it—it would be over. Then something happened which has forever impacted my life. Here I had been struggling with the concept of whether the Lord really does speak. So hesitantly I sat down at the table and opened the workbook to the very next lesson. The title of it was . . . "God Speaks," and it was the story of Lazarus. If I exchanged the word *mother* for the word *brother*, it was as if God was finally answering me.

Then the Spirit of God began to help me understand something.
It seemed to me as if Jesus had said to Mary and Martha:

"You are exactly right. If I had come, your *mother* would not have died. You know that I could have healed *her*, because you have seen me heal many, many times. If I had come when you asked me to, I would have healed *her*. But, you would have never known any more about Me than you already know. I knew that you were ready for a greater revelation of Me than you have ever known in your life. I wanted you to come to know that I am the resurrection and the life. My refusal and My silence were not rejection. It was an opportunity for Me to disclose to you more of Me than you have ever known."[1]

At that moment I realized God was in fact answering me. I knew that over the previous months of intense Bible study and prayer I had developed a truly close relationship with Christ. And he was right; if my mother had not become ill, I probably would have never developed my daily walk with Jesus. It was also probably her death, as difficult as that had been, which had kept me trying to figure out about this God—whom I realized I did not really know. I have a feeling that if God had healed my mother, I would have said, "Thank you very much," and then would have put God back in a box and up on the shelf. Then the next time I had a crisis in my life I would know what I needed to do to get God to perform, but in the meantime, I would be back to handling life on my own. Yet, I came to understand it was because of the loss of my mother and the ensuing struggles that I came to really know and understand God.

Though I was crushed about the loss of my mother, I realized that out of the greatest tragedy of my life had come the greatest blessing—the opportunity to really come to know Christ Jesus as the Lord of my life. It was in that instant I understood what a truly amazing God we worship! Though things do not always go as we expect, God is right with us every step of the way. I recognized—at that moment—that what I wanted to do more than anything was to share with others about the glory of the Lord. I understood without a doubt my purpose in life was to be in full-time ministry. I knew I could help others understand we really do have a God who loves us dearly and is actively involved in our lives.

Reflection Question:

When have you heard God speak to you?

1. Henry Blackaby and Claude King, *Experiencing God: Knowing and Doing the Will of God* (Nashville: LifeWay, 1996), 94.

Divine Encounter 3

With God's Help

I REMEMBER THE TIME when our family was moving from Houston to Colleyville. This was particularly difficult because it would be the third move in three years. My son, Kevin, had actually already gone to three different high schools and we were about to move again. This would mean that his senior year in high school would be in a brand-new town where he did not know anyone. That is a pretty big hardship for a high school senior.

As a mother I was feeling pretty guilty about my son having to leave all of his old friends and start over again at a new school for his senior year. It was a wonderful career opportunity for my husband and as a family we thought it would be best. Kevin was a good sport about the need to move, but I knew it would not be easy for him.

We were blessed to have an outstanding realtor, Chris Ortegal, handling the Colleyville side. She is this incredibly godly woman who goes above and beyond to help her clients. She has a way of finding out about all areas of your life so that she can best meet the family needs. It was not just her goal to find us a great home; she understood that there were lots of other aspects of a family's life which are impacted by a move. She had met our family and knew we were concerned for our son and anxious to make sure that it was a smooth transition for him.

Chris had gone to a banquet one evening and sat beside a couple that worked with the youth at the First United Methodist Church in Colleyville. (That was probably a God-thing that they happened to meet.) She mentioned to them that she was working with a family that would be moving to the area from Houston who had a son who would be a senior. She asked if they had any suggestions for how he could get connected to other youth in the area during the summer so when school started in the fall it might be easier.

They shared with Chris that they would be taking the church youth group on a couple of mission trips during the summer and that maybe

Kevin could join them for the trips. The information was passed over to us, so we started visiting with the church about Kevin participating.

One of the mission trips was to Galveston, so the group said they would be glad to stop and pick Kevin up as they passed through Houston to head down to Galveston. They had a great week together doing mission work in and around the Galveston area.

However, the second mission trip a couple of weeks later would be in England. Kevin was particularly excited about that one. He had never been to England and so it really sounded great. I was thrilled to see Kevin so happy about having a chance to get to know these young people, and so I wanted to make sure that he could go on both of the trips.

As we visited with the youth directors, they shared vital information with us about the England trip. They had bought the tickets for the trip as a group several months before. The youth director was hoping to be able to go back and add Kevin to the list at the same price. But a couple of days before the trip they got in touch to say they had not been able to include him on the group ticket. He was still welcome to go on the trip, but only if I could get him on the same flight as the rest of the group. The youth director mentioned that he was afraid it might be tough as it looked like the plane was almost full, and the remaining tickets were pretty expensive. I said I thought I could get him on and so I began working on it.

To be honest, I thought this would be a pretty easy thing to do. I knew several executives who worked for the airline, as I had served with them on the Chamber of Commerce and other community events. The trip was only a couple of days away; I really needed to get this resolved. However, it seemed all of my contacts were either not available or those I did reach had difficulty trying to help. I started feeling desperate and discouraged.

After several hours of calls, I realized it was hopeless getting Kevin on that flight and thus there was no way he could go on the trip. I sat down on the floor and cried, my heart breaking for my son. He had been so excited and now I needed to figure out how I could tell him the disappointing news. I started praying that God would give me wisdom as to how to break the news to Kevin in hopes that he would not be too upset and disappointed. And then I heard this whisper. I'm not sure where it came from or if it really was in fact audible, but I knew it was God and I heard it clearly. Have you ever had such an experience where you really feel God is whispering in your ear? The voice said, "Call the reservation line." That was ridiculous! I had already called my executive friends and they had tried to pull strings to get Kevin on the flight and it had not worked, so why would I think that calling the reservation line would help? But then I heard it again, "Call the reservation line." I figured, what do I have to lose?

I stood up, picked up the phone, and called the airline. When a random agent answered, I gave her the flight number and asked if there were any seats available on the flight for that date. She did some checking and then came back on the line and said that she was sorry, but that flight was sold out.

I thanked her for her assistance and was about to hang up when all of a sudden I heard her say, "Wait a minute. One just became available." My heart jumped. I knew it would probably be incredibly expensive, but I was willing to pay whatever the price just so Kevin could go. I asked her about it and mentioned it was for my son so he could go on a mission trip with a church.

"Oh, if it is for a student then we might have a student discount ticket," she said as she clicked away on her computer. (I just wanted a ticket for him, but if God wanted to give it to us at a better price, I was certainly open for the blessing.) A few minutes later she told me the price of the student ticket, and it was actually cheaper than what the church had paid for the group tickets several months before. I couldn't believe my ears. I said I would take it.

And by the way, another blessing was that when she assigned Kevin the last seat it just so happened, he was sitting beside one of the other young people from the mission trip! Wow! God is good.

You know, thinking back on that event, what I realized was that I had jumped in trying to get the ticket without ever once asking God about it or seeking his guidance. I was just so convinced that I could do it all on my own. After all, I had lots of friends with the airline who could help me—I didn't think I needed any help from God.

Why do we do that? Why do we decide that we can handle everything in life on our own, and we only talk to God when it is an emergency? God wants to be a part of every moment of our lives, even the little ones. And when God is involved, then he can guide us and direct us in the way that he wants us to go.

You know, God is with us *all* the time—so why don't we do all things with God's help!

Reflection Question:

When have you felt helped by God?

Divine Encounter 4

Kissing Toes

I TRULY BELIEVE THAT God's holy presence is all around us, and if we would only open our eyes, we would recognize the Lord's grace in our everyday experiences. This is why my favorite question to ask myself, as well as others, is "Where have you seen God?"

I particularly love to watch people and see how they connect and support each other and demonstrate their love. I see God in those opportunities to reach out and touch each other's lives. Often when we think about two people being in love, we imagine a young couple getting married and beginning their life together. But I also enjoy watching those who have been married for a while and how they do the little things for each other, such as bringing a spouse a cup of coffee, opening a door, pulling out a chair, or reaching for their hand.

When my mother was struggling with cancer and the effects of chemo, she would often sit in the easy chair in the den of their house. Her lips were so swollen and her mouth was so sensitive with sores from the medicine that it was painful for her to talk or eat. My dad would lie on the sofa near her and he would reach his foot over so it touched hers. They would laugh that it was their way of kissing—with kissing toes. It was this beautiful connection after almost forty-six years of marriage. I could see God in their tender care and love for one another.

There is something beautiful about seeing couples hold on to each other; particularly those who have a long-term relationship. They demonstrate their continuing love and respect as they reach for one another. At one of the churches where I was a pastor, we were putting together a sermon series about what it took to have a strong marriage. We interviewed several couples to see what had made their relationship stronger. They all had wonderful advice. Don't go to bed angry. Always kiss goodbye and hello, regardless of how you feel. Look each other in the eye when you talk.

One particular interview that touched me more than any of the others was an older couple who had been married almost sixty years. It was not what they said that was so powerful. Instead, what really stood out about this adorable couple was how they still looked at each other with such love. As the camera recorded their interview, it did not matter which one of them was speaking, the silent partner would sit there and look at their spouse with incredible admiration, fascination, and pride. They shyly sat on the couch holding hands as the camera recorded their interview. Their hands clasping together was not for the camera and the perceived audience, they authentically cared for each other and expressed it. I had noticed when they sat in church or Sunday School or when someone said, "Let us pray," they would reach for each other. I had often noticed them holding hands when they walked in the parking lot. Despite the many years of marriage, they still held on to each other as a beautiful demonstration of God moving in their lives.

There are many ways to express love and care for others. Keep your eyes open and look to see how people around you use their words and actions to demonstrate affection. You may see actions which touch you deeply. By doing this you might learn new ways of expressing your own heart.

I do not always know the stories behind couples reaching out to each other, and I must be a romantic because I love to imagine what their life must be like together. For example, one Saturday morning I had gotten up to go for a run. A neighbor was having a garage sale and I ran past several parked cars. There was a couple walking down the street toward the garage sale. I noticed them because the gentleman had come around and opened the door for his beloved wife, helped her out of the car, and they then continued walking down the street holding hands. As I passed, I said hello and they greeted me back. I remember thinking what a sweet couple they were. I admired the obvious affection they felt for each other and loved the idea of them spending their Saturday morning enjoying each other's company.

At the end of my run I was surprised to see the same couple walking away from the garage sale. I was amazed that they had been there that long and then I noticed that the man was carrying something in his left hand. As I got closer, I realized that it was a spatula that he was holding. Since it was still fairly early, I imagined that they would now go home and have a romantic breakfast of pancakes, and they could use their new spatula to flip the pancakes. It all looked so beautiful in my imagination. As I came up from behind and started to pass them again, I nodded toward the spatula and asked, "Pancakes?" They both laughed and he said, "Cat litter." Oh well, maybe things aren't always as romantic as you imagine. I could still see God working in their relationship though.

Reflection Question:

How have you seen God demonstrated in relationships?

Divine Encounter 5

Talking to God

WE ALL HAVE DIFFERENT ways of praying. Probably whatever we grew up with is what we feel the most comfortable doing. And sometimes we don't even recognize that there might be other ways of approaching God until we see and hear how someone else does it.

I have a precious friend named Mary Sykes. She is one of those individuals who has this inspiring joy about her and an excitement for life. In fact, as I sit and think about her, I can still hear her laughter as she would enthusiastically tell some story or giggle about her latest adventure. Mary and I were at Foundry United Methodist Church together. She was part of that delightful group of women who met weekly in which we asked the question, "Where have you seen God?" Mary was raised in the Northeast and attended a different religious denomination as a child. At some point she moved to Texas and married Joe Sykes, and they became members of the United Methodist Church. She shared that one of the biggest surprises after she came to Texas was how we prayed. She said that she called home to her mother and exclaimed, "You're not going to believe this, but they make up their own prayers!" For someone who was used to reading prayers from a book, she was shocked that anyone could say whatever they would like to God.

Mary grew to cherish the idea that God heard all of our prayers—whether they were well-crafted liturgy or the ramblings of our heart. And maybe that is one of the things I love about praying to God—that the Lord is accessible. I can pray to God any place and any time! I don't have to go through a priest or preacher to carry my prayers to the Lord. I can read beautifully written prayers or can just talk to God using my own words. I can pray out loud or silently think my prayers. Isn't that amazing! The Lord God Almighty, the King of kings and Lord of lords, loves us so much that we can pray directly to the Creator of the Universe. And even though Jesus has given us some samples of prayers that we can use such as The Lord's Prayer, God is just as willing to hear us when we simply talk from the heart about everything that is happening and what is on our mind.

I have a sweet friend in England who started coming to church and getting more involved in the services and activities. She was a humble, gentle soul who sincerely gave of herself for others and quietly worked in the background. At one point she was asked to pray for our little group that was meeting. She was nervous about praying out loud for the very first time. She had never spoken her prayers so others could hear them. We encouraged her and told her that in whatever way she expressed her prayers they would be great. She needed to remember God loved her and we loved her so if she decided she wanted to pray out loud then her words, if coming from the heart, would be just right. She definitely wanted to be the one to pray, and so we bowed our heads. I remember how touched I was when she began by saying, "Lord, this is Edith, . . ." and then went on from there. It was so simple and unassuming, as if acknowledging that God has a lot of prayers to hear and maybe it would be polite to introduce oneself first so that the Lord knows who is talking.

It was a wonderful reminder for me that God already knows us. How does the Lord keep up with everyone and all the different prayer requests? (Though I guess if it has been a while since we have talked to God, we may feel like we need to reintroduce ourselves.) In addition to knowing who we are, God knows absolutely everything about us and what we are thinking. Yet the Divine still wants to hear what is on our hearts. Are you willing to open up and just talk with God like you would a good friend?

By the way, God doesn't just want to hear from us when there is a problem and we need help. Think about being a parent. Would you only want to hear from your child when they need your assistance? What if they totally ignored you all the rest of the time, but then when they had a problem, then all of a sudden you can expect them to call and tell you what a great parent you are and . . . oh by the way, can they borrow the car or can you give them some money or help them with their problem? You would still love them because they are your child, but you would probably feel pretty hurt by the fact that it felt like they were just using you. Might God feel the same way when we avoid praying except when we need help? The Lord wants to be involved in every aspect of our lives and to truly be in a relationship with us.

We have a God who loves us dearly and wants us to "pray continually"[1] and be in a relationship with him. And, guess what, it really is OK if we make up our prayers and tell God everything that is on our mind.

Reflection Question:

How do you pray to God?

1. 1 Thess 5:17.

Divine Encounter 6

You Have to Look Up to See Rainbows

WHEN I THINK ABOUT where I have seen God, I am often reminded of some of the remarkable individuals I have had the pleasure of calling my friends. Each of them has a unique life with his or her own share of joys and sorrows and unbelievable experiences. There are some friendships that just quietly grow stronger as you get to know each other and then there are those individuals who blow you away from the first moment you meet them. Pat Dahnke falls into that latter category.

Pat and I met at 6:30 a.m. on a Thursday morning at the Ritz Carlton Hotel. We both happened to attend a networking breakfast for the first time on the same day and sat beside each other at the visitor's table. It was a group called Women's Business Support Network, or better known simply as WBSN. We had been instructed to share our stories around the table and figure out if there were ways that we could support each other.

The story Pat shared that morning touched me deeply and has forever been a reminder to me of how God reveals himself to us. Pat began telling her story of the picture-perfect life. She had a great marriage, three wonderful children, and was the owner of a small chain of dress shops. Then her ideal life hit a wall. Her youngest son, Kent, a beautiful blonde haired and blue-eyed two-and-a-half-year-old, started complaining about an earache and a stomach ache. When they finally found out what was going on, it was too late. He was diagnosed with a tumor and the scary official word of neuroblastoma. They could treat it with chemotherapy and help with the pain, but the long-term prognosis was not good.

Pat shared about the next few months of Kent being in and out of the hospital and how they tried to make every moment a time of joy for him. He loved to color and even at that young age he was good at drawing rainbows, lots and lots of rainbows. His favorite TV show was *Rainbow Brite*, about a little girl who would ride her colorful pony over the rainbow. Kent and Kelley, a fourteen-year-old friend who was also in the hospital, would fill each other's rooms with pictures of rainbows. They even had a fifty-foot kite tail that stretched throughout the room which made the doctors' and nurses' approach slower, but happier as they stepped over the bright rainbow colors.

At one point between chemotherapy treatments, Pat had to fly from Houston to Dallas for business. While on the plane she had earnestly prayed to God about Kent's health. She was desperate to know that God was hearing her prayers. When she opened her eyes and looked out the window, she saw the most gorgeous rainbow she had ever seen. She felt a tremendous amount of peace. She did not know if God would heal her son, but she knew God was with him and with her and that she could trust the Lord.

A month or two later the doctors told Pat that Kent did not have much longer to live. As she sat by his bed, she tried to figure out how you could possibly explain heaven to a small child. Death is a tough topic for adults to understand, but how do you help a two-and-a-half-year-old understand that God will be with them and that it will all be OK. As she sat there in silence struggling with what to say, Kent looked up at her and said, "Mom, I'm going to ride the rainbow with Rainbow Brite." Yes! What a perfect explanation. She hugged him and agreed and told him how much fun it would be and that he would be feeling great, knowing inside she would have the greatest loss in her life.

Later at Kent's memorial service there was a rainbow. Some people may have thought it was the light playing off of the stained-glass windows, but for those who really noticed this glorious display of light, they knew it was a sign. However, Pat had not seen it, so when they got back to her house after the service and all of these people kept commenting about the rainbow, Pat was devastated. She was his mother and she needed to see that rainbow. It would have meant so very much to her, almost as if it were a sign from Kent to her. But she missed it.

The next day, as they drove from Texas to Kansas to bury Kent in her hometown of Emporia, Pat started sobbing. She was so upset about losing her child, but also about not seeing the rainbow at the funeral. All of a sudden, she looked out the window to the right and there was a rainbow. She very clearly heard Kent's precious little voice say, "Mommy, yesterday you were too sad, you have to look up to see the rainbows."

What a beautiful reminder to Pat and to all of us—"You have to look up to see the rainbows." That phrase would be engraved on Kent's tombstone. But it is also a phrase that is engraved on many hearts that have heard this story.

That is not the end of the story. Kent's friend Kelley went into a coma about six weeks after Kent died. Pat went up to the hospital to see her and

her mother. On her way back home from the hospital it had been rain-
ing yet the sun was shining. Pat kept thinking there should be a rainbow
somewhere in the sky. She stopped the car five or six times and just stood
in the rain looking for a rainbow, but never saw one. When she reached her
house about thirty minutes later, there was a beautiful rainbow in the sky
back toward the medical center area. She was so struck by its beauty that
she could barely walk. A neighbor saw her outside and came out to share
the spectacular view. Then Pat ran in to call Kelley's mom so that she could
look out the window of the hospital to see it. At first the nurse said that she
could not come to the phone, so Pat just asked that a message about the
rainbow be passed to her, but soon Shirley, Kelley's mom, picked up the
phone and she asked when the rainbow had appeared. Pat said it was about
fifteen minutes ago. And she was told, "That's when Kelley passed." Pat went
outside and sat for about two more hours knowing that she had witnessed
one of the most wonderful feats on earth. God is amazing!

As Pat shared her story something deep inside of me was touched.
My heart ached for her and her loss. As a mother, I could not imagine the
pain of watching your young child go through something so difficult. I was
amazed how strong this woman was as she witnessed to God being with
her through all that she had experienced. It truly opened my eyes to how
God can use natural events, such as the rainbow, to touch us so deeply with
perfect timing.

Since then there have been numerous perfectly timed rainbows on
the anniversaries of Kent's and Kelley's deaths, and on Kent's birthday. At
first, Pat would look for them on those days, but as the years passed, she
would often forget until she saw a rainbow and then she would remember
what the day was. The first few years she said that she felt like she needed
to see those rainbows to foster her trust in God. For a grieving mother it
was truly a sign from both Kent and God saying that it was OK. As time
progressed, she realized that she was not desperate for them, they were
blessings, little gifts from God.

One year she happened to be in Arizona on one of those special days
and it was a sunny bright day. She thought that because of the weather there
was no way she would see a rainbow that day. And at that moment she looked
up to see a rainbow hot air balloon floating effortlessly through the sky. She
laughed to think that even on a day when there was no rain that God was
gracious enough to send her a rainbow in a totally different way.

Pat and I would go on to become very close friends. I have watched
her through the years, and I am still amazed at her faith, her talent, and
how hard she works. She ended up becoming a fashion designer and her
business, Designs by Pat, has won numerous awards. She owns a ranch in

Waller, Texas, where she has her design studio and factory, along with where her beautiful daughter, Tara, raises and trains horses. And the ranch has the perfect name—Rainbow Ranch.

As I was writing this book, I got a call from Pat sharing that she had been in Santa Fe having dinner with some friends and something wonderful happened. Her friend got up during the meal to go outside and check on something in his car. When he came back in, he told Pat about a spectacular rainbow. (He knew her story.) She went running out to see it. It did not last long, about five minutes, but it was magnificent. And then she remembered what day it was—August 17—Kent's birthday! She had not even thought about what the day was and to be looking for a rainbow, yet God surprised her and reminded her with a colorful whisper, "I am with you!" And guess what, God is with each of us as well.

Reflection Question:

Where have you seen God in nature?

Divine Encounter 7

Obeying the Whisper

THERE ARE TIMES IN my life when I have heard a voice or a whisper and somehow deep in my soul, I have known it was God. Usually those times when I have realized it was God is when it is something that is completely out of the blue and I am not expecting it. It is often something that I would never think of on my own such as an instruction that does not make sense to me.

There are also those times when I seem to hear a whisper to do something that seems like a logical thing to do . . . if I were really a nice person. Some of those whispers may be from God as well, or it may also be my conscience, or thinking what my saintly mother would want me to do. Either way, I have learned that it is important to obey those whispers—even if it is not something that I really want to do. For instance, those times when you may have felt an urge or a nudge to call and check on someone that you had not even been thinking about, only to find out that it was perfect timing for them needing to hear an encouraging word. Or maybe it was an invisible push to go help a stranger that you see struggling with something. You might have preferred to keep doing whatever you were doing and not get involved, but after you listened to that whisper and obeyed you realize how important it was to give assistance.

A good example of this occurred one morning when I was out running before dawn, and it happened to be trash day. As I passed through the streets of one of the neighborhoods, it was apparent that a dog or a raccoon or something had been out the night before. It was particularly evident on one of the streets where almost every trash can had been knocked down, and it looked like something had scrounged through all the trash.

The moment I started to turn down that street I saw the mess. It was still dark, but from the light of the streetlights it looked like rubbish scattered all over the street and yards. My temptation as soon as I saw it was to turn around and run in another area. There was certainly no reason I had to go down this particular street. After all, every morning I would go a different route so that

I could pray for the houses on whatever street I was running. I would just redirect my prayers, and my run, to a different street.

But then I heard it—that whisper that said for me to clean it up. Or maybe I sensed it . . . or just knew it was the right thing to do. I knew that if the people woke up and saw all of this mess, it would throw their morning routines into chaos. They probably put their trash cans out at nighttime thinking that was one less thing they had to do in the morning while they were rushing to get children off to school and themselves to work.

Believe me it was not something I wanted to do. Oh goodness, stinky garbage! What if someone looked out their window and saw me walking around in the dark in their yard? They might think I was a burglar or that I had made all of this mess. Besides, I didn't really have time for this. I needed to finish my run and get to work myself. This wasn't my problem!

But I had heard the whisper and I knew I had to do it. So, for the next twenty minutes, in the dark I walked up and down this street setting up trash cans and picking up trash and making sure that the street and every yard looked good. No one ever drove by and no one ever came out of their house. It was just me and the stars . . . and God, working to make the street look better. In the end it became a matter of pride to make sure every last scrap of paper and the coffee grounds and chewed up chicken bones were picked up and put back into the cans. My hands had been covered in yuk (that is the technical term) and I had wiped them on my running clothes several times, and so I felt like I looked and smelled like the rubbish that I had just been picking up. But in the end, I felt like I had done a good job. And I knew no one else would ever know what had been done, but God would. In fact, the whole time I was picking up the trash I was saying over and over, "Whatever you do, work at it with all your heart."[1]

As the sun began to rise and I took one last look at the perfectly clean street, I had a smile on my face. I ran down the street a final time and prayed for each house and headed home. No one ever knew, but I did. And though it definitely was not something I wanted to do, in the end I was glad I did it.

Maybe it was good for me to get my hands dirty and to do something I did not want to do. If nothing else, it taught me the importance of obeying when you get that whisper.

Unfortunately, there have also been those times when I knew that God was telling me to do something, and yet I did not immediately do it. Those times when I have not obeyed, I would often rationalize why it was OK for me to ignore those God-whispers. I would try to convince myself that God probably did not know how busy I was with other important things. Surely

---

1. Col 3:23.

the Lord would not have asked me to interrupt *my* plans to handle this request (as if we think we know better than God about what is really important)!

For example, I remember a time during the Houston Marathon when my husband was running, and I was there to cheer for him and support him. He had been training for months and I was so proud of him. I had studied the race route, and we had decided on several key places where I would attempt to be in order to cheer him on and to be available in case he needed anything such as Gatorade, energy gel, or more socks.

The race had begun in downtown Houston, and I waved to him from the starting line. I knew the runners would run north for a couple of miles and then would circle back through the main streets of downtown before heading out the south side. The plan was for me to meet him on a certain corner when they came back through downtown. The rendezvous place was about ten blocks west of the start of the race. To be honest, I had lots of time to get to that particular location, but I was not sure how fast he would be running, and I did not want to miss him. Not that he would really need anything at this point in the race, but I wanted to be there for him and give him a cheer of encouragement.

I started heading across the parking lots and streets to where I would meet him and as I went by a vacant lot, I passed a homeless man sitting on the curb and he appeared to be reading a Bible. I was surprised to see him there and probably even more surprised to see him reading a Bible. And that is when I heard it, the whisper . . . "Ask him if he understands what he is reading."

I began arguing with God in my mind. "Seriously Lord, this sounds like the book of Acts and the story of Philip and the Ethiopian.[2] You don't really expect me to sit down and talk with him. I have someplace I need to be. Besides, he looks like he is doing just fine."

And I kept feeling like I was supposed to sit down and visit with him, yet that is not what I wanted to do . . . and that is not what I did. Instead, I convinced myself that it was much more important that I get over to the appointed street corner and wait for my husband so that I could cheer him on. And I told the Lord, "I'll be glad to visit with the man when I come back, but not now, Lord, not now."

Sometimes God just gives us one shot at getting something right and once we pass up that opportunity, we never get it again. I made it to the corner where I watched all the runners pass and it was probably a good forty-five minutes to an hour before I ever had the brief opportunity just to

2. Acts 8:26–40.

wave at my husband as he smiled and kept on running. And the entire time I stood there it was eating me alive that I should have stopped.

As soon as my husband passed, I sprinted back to that vacant lot hoping that the homeless man was still there. I was ready to sit down and visit with him and would be delighted to explain the Bible, if needed. Only when I got there . . . he was nowhere to be seen. I had missed my opportunity.

It may not seem like a big deal, but that event, which was over thirty years ago, still haunts me. I know God called me to witness to that man, to just sit down and talk with him, to see if he understood what he was reading in the Bible. And I missed the opportunity.

Bottom line is this: God speaks to us either in an audible voice or a whisper or a nudge that points us toward doing something which is the Lord's will. It is a privilege and an honor to be able to serve the Lord. The important thing is to be obedient, even when it is something we don't want to do. We don't always know how it will turn out, but God does. And something inside of us changes when we are obedient; it is as if we move a step closer to the Lord and maybe see things through divine eyes. And in the same respect, when we disobey the Lord and refuse to do what is wanted, then it seems to put a distance between us and the Lord and hurts our relationship.

I don't know about you, but I want to see God and hear God and grow closer than ever to God. I realize that my obedience is a big factor in how strong our relationship is. I also have come to realize that when I am obedient, then it makes it much easier to see God working around me and to hear his voice when he does whisper to me.

Reflection Question:

In what ways have you obeyed God's whisper?

Divine Encounter 8

Falling Star

I FIND MYSELF OFTEN reflecting on that life-altering morning a few months after my mother's passing. I was reading in my *Experiencing God* workbook when I knew that God was speaking to me and letting me know through Jesus' words that he was aware of what I was going through and was right there with me. It was in that moment that I realized that God truly is actively involved in our lives. In my heart I comprehended that the most important thing I could do with my life was to go into full-time ministry and spend the rest of my life sharing about the God who loves us and is always right there beside us.

I recognized that like me, most people just saw life through their own eyes and were not aware of how the Lord is constantly with us and wants to have a relationship with us. I had heard those words before, but prior to that moment it had not clicked for me that there was a way to live your life fully in the presence of God. When you are constantly aware of God with you and guiding you, then it makes a difference in how you look at life and experience what is going on around you. There is amazing hope and an excitement and a recognition that there is a higher level of living. I wanted more than anything to share about God with others and it seemed the best way to do that was as a preacher, pastor, and minister.

I had no idea what it really took to become a minister, yet I trusted that God would open the door for me when the timing was right. In the meantime, I had an insatiable hunger for learning more about Jesus Christ. So, I became even more involved in my church by teaching and serving in leadership positions. I traveled to the Holy Land a couple of times and did extensive research on the various places we had visited. I kept praying that the Lord would show me where I was to serve. And I considered thoughts about how to leave my career to pursue whatever God called me to do.

Every so often, I would be compelled to share with my husband about feeling the need to go into the ministry. I could tell he was not as thrilled as I about the idea. It would certainly be a big change for our family. We both had good careers, our lifestyle was built on a two-career marriage and it would mean some adjustments for all of us. I knew this was not a decision to be made lightly. I continued to trust in God's timing, knowing if this deep desire I was feeling about being in full-time ministry was really from God, then it would become obvious when to step away from my wonderful career with Southwestern Bell Telephone. I was sure everything would fall into place.

After five years of waiting for God to show me where and how I was to serve; and not feeling any closer to understanding my call, I was feeling a deep frustration. As much as I loved my career in the telecommunications business, I was willing to walk away from it, if only God would let me know what to do and how to move forward.

On February 28, 2001, my prayer to God was, "Lord, if you want me to serve you full-time, then either show me where or kick me out of this job. Otherwise I guess you want me to just keep working for Southwestern Bell and serving you on the side. But I am tired of feeling like I need to be serving you in a bigger way and yet not knowing how to get there!"

Two days later I was out of town at a legal conference when I received an early morning phone call from my secretary. She was letting me know that I had a 9:30 a.m. conference call with the president of our subsidiary. I slipped out of the conference a few minutes before the call and went to my hotel room where I could focus on what was being said. I had a feeling there was a connection to my prayer a few days earlier and so I prayed before the call, "Lord, I don't know what this is about, but if there is some way that it would open a door for me to go into ministry . . . then I'm ready."

The call was about our subsidiary reorganizing and that I needed to get back to the office so that we could pull all the management employees together after lunch to let them know what was going on and then be ready to meet with all of the other employees. It would mean they were offering early retirement for those that qualified. I wasn't sure if I had enough years to take the early retirement, but I got excited thinking that maybe this was God's way of giving me an opportunity to go into ministry. I also realized that if I had left prior to this that I would have walked away with nothing, yet if it did work out that I could take early retirement, that even though I could not touch it now, in the future it would be waiting for me or at least be benefits for my family. I rushed back to the home office and handled the meetings and then wondered what God would do next.

That weekend we had company and lots of things going on, so my husband and I never really had a chance to discuss things. He knew about the announcement, but I was anxious to talk with him about my figuring out a way to go ahead and leave my career. It was not a conversation I wanted to have casually, instead I really wanted us to sit down and talk.

On Monday evenings my son and I went to Bible Study Fellowship (better known as BSF) classes at a church near our home. I knew we would not get back until late and so I decided to hold off on the discussion until Tuesday evening. Besides, my son would be working at Starbucks on Tuesday night, so I figured it was a good time for my husband and me to just sit down together and talk everything through. It would be a big decision for us.

Now you need to understand up front that I don't cook. Actually, I can cook, but I am not very confident about it. But if I decide I really want to talk about something important, then I'll cook a big meal. So that was what I did on Tuesday. I had really prayed about it and felt with everything going on at work that this could be the right time to leave my career and go into ministry and so I wanted everything perfect as my husband and I visited about it. I had gone to the grocery store (another one of those things I do not like to do) and bought all the good stuff and had come home to make a fancy meal. The table was all set and lots of food prepared when he came home. It probably scared him when he walked in the door because it was obvious that I had something important to discuss.

We sat down and started the meal and I began the conversation by explaining that for five years I had felt that God was calling me to the ministry and that now with the changes at my company, it looked like it might be a great time to leave and begin the process of becoming a minister. I knew it would mean some big changes for us and I would not do it if he did not agree, but I truly believed that was what I should do. And I waited for his reply.

He shocked me by saying, "I agree, I think that is what you need to do." (Oh, my goodness, after five years he is finally agreeing—what joy!) But then he went on to say, "But we will need to sell the house, and you need to know that I am leaving you." He folded up his napkin, stood up, said he was going for a drive, and walked out.

I sat there in stunned silence for what felt like an eternity. It was as if I was afraid to move. I could not breathe. My heart was pounding in my chest and my head felt like it was swimming and dizzy. I could not think straight, and it felt like I was being bombarded with questions and fear and panic. What just happened? Did my husband really say that he was walking away from our marriage, our life that we had built together? Was this all just because I felt called to go into the ministry? I was in shock! I knew our marriage was not perfect, but we never fought, and I thought he loved me. I knew that I definitely loved him.

The next couple of days were like a fog. I went to work, but between my trying to figure out what was going on with my marriage and the chaos around work, it was pretty crazy. I had made a few calls just to see if I was even eligible for the early retirement. Apparently, I shocked some people that I would even consider it. I received a call from the Engineering Department to see if I might be interested in coming to their organization and was told it would even be a promotion and more money. That just added to the confusion. Was this God's way of saving my marriage and blessing us financially?

By Thursday evening I was totally confused. I thought I had always been a pretty reasonable person who could figure out a creative solution to any situation and yet now it was as if I could not gather my thoughts and make sense of all that was going on. Life seemed to be crumbling all around me and yet I could not react to it to stop the chaos and bewilderment in which I was drowning. I knew I needed to make several major decisions, but it seemed like everything was just this mixed-up mess of issues. I could not think straight about how to even begin to know what was right. I went to bed that night but could not sleep. Finally, about 2 a.m., I decided to get up. I knew it was supposed to be a full moon so I thought I would go sit by the pool and pray that God would give me some divine guidance as to what I needed to do. We had a swing on the patio, so I took a quilt and went out in the dark to sit there all wrapped up and enjoying the quiet to pray. But I was disappointed when I looked up into the night sky—there were clouds covering everything so you could not see the moon or the stars. I wanted clarity and precision as to what to do and yet the thick cloudy, dreary sky mirrored my brain and my dull, confused thoughts. It was a feeling of suffocating under the burden of too many perplexing issues.

I began talking to God, "Oh Lord, I really wanted to see the moon. I just need to talk to you, and I guess I thought if I could see the moon and the stars that I would feel closer to you. Lord, you know that I want to do what you want me to do, but if I don't know your will then how can I do it? Lord, if you would just make it very clear to me, I would appreciate it. If you would just clear away the clouds and line up the stars to spell it all out for me—'Keva, on item number one do this . . .' But I know that is not how you work. So, if I could just talk with you about everything that is going on, maybe I will know what you want me to do."

And I began with the first issue—my marriage. And as I sat there and thought about it, I realized that even though I had thought before that it was connected to all of my other decisions, I realized it was not. When it came to whether I wanted my marriage to last, that wasn't even a question for me. Of course, I wanted my marriage to last. This was the man I wanted to grow old with. I loved him dearly. I wasn't sure what was going on, but I realized this issue was not my decision. I voted yes to stay in the marriage, but it took both of us and I realized he would have to decide whether he would stay. So, all I could do on this issue was to place it back into God's hands and trust that the Lord's will would be done. It seems like sometimes that is all you can do.

But I did have a decision to make on the second issue, which was whether I took the early retirement and went into ministry, or to take the promotion and the engineering job and continue with my career. As much as I loved my career and would have enjoyed the engineering opportunity, all I could think about was that for the last five years I had really felt that God was calling me into ministry. I felt like I had to preach and share about this amazing God. As I sat there and weighed the two options, it became very clear that I needed to take the early retirement and figure out what I should do to go into ministry so that I could preach.

From that point on, as I sat in the swing and stared up at the sky, I took all the other issues which had previously seemed wrapped around each other. One by one I was able to separate each one, look at all the options available for that particular issue, and then decide how to move forward. It was amazing how everything seemed to be so clear. I could imagine the different opportunities and options for my personal issues, as well as how to handle my organization and staff. And I felt like God was giving me wisdom as to what I needed to do in every area.

After a while I had gone through all of the issues and decisions that I needed to make, and I truly felt that on each one God had given me discernment and direction as to what the next step should be. It was the most astounding feeling of clarity and insight and vision. I sat back and just sighed. It felt like a huge weight had just been lifted off my shoulders and that the fog in my mind had cleared. I prayed and said, "Lord, I think you have answered me on all of these issues, and you have shown me the way I need to go. But please, Lord, if I have not understood you correctly in any of these areas, then please stop me before I go down the wrong path. Close the door so I don't go against what you want. You know my heart and you know I desperately want to do your will."

About that time the clouds began to clear. They parted in the middle so that I could see behind them the most beautiful full moon I have ever seen in my life! It was huge and silver and I almost felt that I could reach out and touch it. It was spectacular as it was framed with the dark clouds. I just stared at the moon in awe and began to laugh, "Oh, thank you, Lord, it is beautiful! Thank you for showing me your moon. I love it!" And then as an afterthought, I kiddingly added, "But you forgot the stars." And at that moment, directly below the moon there was a falling star!

I sat there in total amazement feeling incredibly blessed. It was as if it were a check mark, and God was saying, "I hear your prayer, I am with you, and I will always be with you!"

That night set the stage for the rest of my life. It was a personal reminder that God hears our prayers and will guide us, if we only listen. I would love to say that my marriage worked out, but it did not. Though I loved him dearly and had always imagined that we would grow old together, my husband was in love with someone else. Actually, they are happily married now. He is a good man. He just decided that he did not want to be married to me anymore.

It was heart wrenching to lose the love of my life, yet God has a way of reminding us that we are never alone, and we are in fact loved. Even if it may not be the stereotypical version we always pictured from when we were little. We have this view of the perfect family and the white picket fence around the house. And sometimes God says he has bigger things for us, which means stepping beyond the previous boundaries and going places, seeing things, and meeting people we never imagined. It is astounding the number of opportunities God has opened up for me and I am beyond blessed to serve the Lord in ministry. My heart is bursting for all the precious people I have had the privilege of coming to know as I have traveled throughout the world, lived in various places, served in different churches, and preached to all sizes of congregations. And what I realize is that sometimes God calls us to be willing to go and do whatever is required to serve him. Often that begins by holding lightly to the things, places, and even people who might restrict you from being able to give your all to the Lord. It has been the greatest adventure ever to allow God to direct my steps and open up incredible ministry opportunities. It is so marvelously obvious that God is involved and active in our lives when we make Jesus Christ the focus and the Lord of everything we think, say, and do.

By the way, one other thing, I do find it interesting that every once in a while, I have someone mention that they don't believe that women should preach and be in ministry. When they say that I just smile and think to myself about the night when I had a choice of ministry or doing something else with my life. And I know without a doubt that it was the Lord God Almighty who directed my steps that night . . . and continues to do so.

Reflection Question:

When have you experienced God giving you a sign?

Seminary Life

Divine Encounter 9

Sharing a Part of Me

I ALWAYS STAND AMAZED at how God puts things in place. Sometimes we have the privilege to recognize that God is moving in a powerful way, and we can look back to see the events that have led to that extraordinary event. It is often a whole conglomeration of God-things that have opened doors and guided you step by step until you reach that particular instant in time. They all seem like unrelated events as you experience them, and yet later you know they were more than just random activities. Instead you realize they were a beautiful weaving of experiences that have directed you on the path until you reach the place where you know God has brought you.

In 2001, I knew I had to go into the ministry full time. By this point, I was finally figuring out what it took to become a minister. To be honest, before that time I knew God had called me to preach, but I did not know what it took to become a minister in a church. I thought that since God was calling me to that role that somehow some group of people would just recognize I would be a good preacher, and they would come tap me on the shoulder and invite me to preach to them. It didn't exactly happen like that. Instead I realized there was a process to go through in the United Methodist Church (which is the denomination I was in when I was called), and that it would be best if I actually went to seminary and did a little studying, so I was better prepared.

I had just begun checking into seminaries when our pastor, Rev. Godfrey Hubert, from our Houston church, came to Dallas for a meeting. We lived in Colleyville at the time, which was near where the meeting would be held, and so we offered for him to stay at our home. Since he knew my heart was to go into the ministry, he invited me to go along with him to the meeting. I had the opportunity to connect with some key individuals who would play important roles in my life. One of them was Dr. William J. Abraham and another was Dr. Stan Copeland. Over lunch that day, Dr. Abraham asked me about my interest in going into ministry and invited me to come visit with him at Perkins School of Theology at Southern Methodist University.

A few days later I met Dr. Abraham at his office and had a wonderful visit about ministry and seminaries. He is a great theologian, and it was a blessing to have him take the time to explain what was involved in theological education and what to look for in choosing a seminary. Since fall classes would be starting soon, he walked me over to the registrar's office. It was really beyond the due date of submitting an application for that semester, but with Dr. Abraham and others' help, I was able to apply and be accepted.

The next week school began. The first day was an orientation and signing up for our different classes. When Dr. Abraham and I had visited, he told me that in the upcoming semester he would be teaching an Intro to Theology course. He had shared that it was a foundational class for the rest of seminary and suggested that if possible that I sign up for his class. I had enjoyed meeting Dr. Abraham and knew he was well respected theologically and so I definitely was looking forward to his class. That first day as we registered for classes, he came to me to let me know his teaching schedule had been changed. He would still be teaching the Intro to Theology course the next semester; however, he would be teaching it in Houston instead of on the Dallas campus. It would be every Monday evening during the fall and a couple of Saturdays. He said he would still love to have me in class, but it would mean either flying or driving four hours to Houston every Monday for an evening class from 6:30 p.m. until 9:00 p.m., and then getting back in the car and driving back home late that night and being ready for my early morning Tuesday classes. Dr. Abraham mentioned he, along with another professor and a grad student, would be flying down each week, renting a car to get to class, and then following the classes would rush back to the airport to catch the last flight back to Dallas. He said I was welcome to travel with them. It was a quicker travel arrangement, but also a more expensive one, especially since I was no longer working, and things were tight financially. But I decided it was worth the money and figured God would help with it, so I decided to go ahead and sign up for the class. It ended up being one of the best decisions I have ever made. Dr. Abraham has the ability to look at the deeper things of God and then to break them down and explain them in a way that opens up your understanding. The information and the foundation I gained from that class were extremely beneficial during the rest of seminary and have also cultivated an inner strength that has fortified my ministry. My deep respect and friendship with Dr. Abraham have been a powerful influence in my life.

But the story does not end there. One Saturday we had class in Houston from about 9:00 a.m. until 3:00 p.m. It meant getting up really early and driving down to Houston. As soon as class was over the plan was to jump back in the car and drive back to Dallas to study and do everything else I had planned for that weekend. However, when I ran to my car after class, I sat down, put my seat belt on, and was just about to start the car when all of a sudden, I heard a voice clearly say, "Do not leave Houston." I froze! Whether it was actually out loud or just in my mind I did not really know, but I did know in that instant that it was God speaking to me. My heart was racing, and I was scared to move. I literally just sat there without shifting an inch, just listening, and my mind was racing. Was there more to the message? Did this really just happen? If I move, am I going to be struck by lightning or possibly lose whatever connection there was in that instant? I sat there in my car without moving for about thirty minutes as I waited for further instructions or some idea of what I was supposed to do.

It finally dawned on me that the instructions were not to leave Houston. That did not mean that I could not move my body in the car or even possibly drive my car somewhere else. I just was not supposed to leave Houston. I had already been worried about how much studying I needed to do in all of my other classes. My plan had been to rush back home to work on everything. But I at least had my books in the car, and so I decided I could drive someplace and study. At least then I would not be wasting time, and I would not be leaving Houston.

When I had lived in Houston, I frequently ran at Memorial Park, so I decided to drive there and study at one of the picnic tables while I waited for God to show me what I was supposed to be doing. I did that for a couple of hours until I started getting hungry. Once again, I thought back on the voice I had heard and the instructions were just that I was not supposed to leave Houston, but it did not say that I could not get something to eat. I decided to drive some place and get some dinner.

While eating I was still trying to figure out what it meant not to leave Houston. Why was I here? What was I supposed to be doing? I remembered there was an Emmaus Walk (a three-day spiritual retreat) that would be going on in the area. Some of my friends from my previous church (Foundry United Methodist in Houston) would be there working on the team. There would be a Saturday evening worship and prayer time. With all that had gone on that afternoon, I really wanted to be in a church somewhere praying and to be surrounded with others who were praying. I decided to drive over to where I thought the Emmaus Walk was being held. I knew after the service was over, I would need to find a place to sleep. It would be way too late to drive back to Dallas. My son was a little over an hour from Houston at College Station. I talked with him right before I went into the service and told him that I might want to come spend the night at his apartment. I would call him later to let him know. In my mind I still was not sure I could leave Houston, but maybe after I spent time in this little church praying then I would know better what I needed to do.

I went inside for the service. It was a great time of worship. Part of what they do is pray for all of the pilgrims and team who are on the three-day retreat. They call them out by name. I recognized the names of some of my friends who I knew would be working on the team, but then all of a sudden, they called out the name of Barbara McDowell. Barbara McDowell! I used to know a Barbara McDowell. But I knew it could not be her. Barbara and I had been in a women's networking group together called the Women's Business Support Network. It was a group of amazing women from all different types of businesses, who got together at 6:30 a.m. every Thursday at the Ritz Carlton Hotel for breakfast, networking, and encouraging each other. Barbara had been the president of the organization when I joined, and I followed her in that position a little later. We had become close during our time in the organization, but then she and her husband, Joel, had moved out to a lake in East Texas and I had not seen her for a while. I really did not think it could be her, but I was curious. One of the team members was at the back of the church so at an opportune moment I went back to ask her what the Barbara McDowell who was on the retreat looked like. She said there were three women named Barbara on the walk, so she was not sure which one was which. I had thought I would slip out of the service early but decided to stick around . . . maybe this was my Barbara and maybe this was why I was supposed to stay in Houston.

In a little while, the pilgrims came in and I had an opportunity to see that it was in fact "my Barbara." My heart jumped when I saw her, and I knew immediately that was why I was there. She caught a glimpse of me and was just as surprised to see me. I had been involved with the Emmaus Walk and had attended both as a pilgrim and several times as a team member, so I knew the schedule and knew we would not have a good opportunity to visit until late Sunday afternoon when the retreat would be ending. But at least now I knew why I had to stay in Houston. I needed to talk with Barbara. I didn't know what was going on that necessitated my visit with her, but at least I knew she was the reason God had told me not to leave.

I ended up walking out of the church and going straight to the car to get my cell phone to call my son. I told him that I knew why I needed to be in Houston and that I needed to stay so would not be spending the night with him. He asked where I was going to stay for the night and I told him I had absolutely no idea, but I knew God would provide. I hung up the phone and looked up and a young couple, Joel and Amy Sykes, who had been from our church there in Houston prior to our moving, were walking up to me.

They were so excited and surprised by my presence. They happened to see me as I left the church and had come out in the parking lot to find me. They immediately asked if I would come spend the night at their house. They had two small children and they said they knew the kids would think it was "like Christmas morning" if they could wake up and find I was at their home. I immediately accepted and was thankful for God's provision.

The next day was a day full of God-moments. I had awakened early only to remember that it was the fall time change and so the clocks had been moved backward. I was up an hour earlier than was needed for church. But as Amy fixed breakfast she told me that Foundry UMC had started another service, so now there were three services on Sunday. When I had lived there and attended that church, I had been very involved in teaching a Sunday School class. Our class would normally meet during the first service and then we would attend the worship service together during the second service. But since I was up so early, I decided to go to the very early morning service and figured I would miss a lot of my friends. Yet when I arrived at church there was all of my Sunday School class sitting in the usual spot. It was so great to see them. They had changed their schedule when the new service was put in place. It was an unexpected blessing to see them all. Plus, when my previous pastor, Godfrey, saw me in the congregation, he invited me to come forward and help serve Holy Communion, which is a sacred thing to do. A little later I went to eat and was delightfully surprised to see my old biking team walk in to eat lunch together. When I had lived in Houston, I would go biking with them on Saturdays and we would ride a long distance together and then all go out to eat together afterward. I was thrilled that they happened to be riding this particular day and I had a chance to see all of them. The day was full of chance meetings where I had the incredible opportunity to see people that I had not seen in the past year since we had moved away from the area. It seemed that everywhere I turned God was blessing me with the privilege to see another friend.

At 4:00 p.m. I headed back out to the Emmaus Retreat. I knew they would be having the closing service and then after it was over then maybe I could say hello to Barbara and visit for just a few minutes. It was a great service and apparently a wonderful spiritual time for all those involved. When it was completed Barbara came rushing back to where I had been seated. The first thing I said as she walked up to me was, "How is your health?"

She looked at me strangely and sort of cocked her head to one side saying, "You know normally, Keva, we say hello before we start asking questions like that, but since you asked, it is not very good. I need a kidney transplant, but Joel will give me one of his kidneys after the first of the year."

My response was, "I don't think that will work out, but I'll be glad to give you one of mine." I have no idea why those words came out of my mouth. It was as if I was speaking, but the words were not from me.

She was truly shocked by my comment and said, "Keva, you don't know what you are talking about. Joel has already gone through lots of testing and everything is set. We are just waiting for insurance issues to be handled so we can go on with the surgery. Why in the world would you say such a thing?"

I answered, "I don't know, but if you need me, I will be here for you."

We quickly changed the subject and started talking about everything that had happened in the last four or five years since they had moved away from Houston and our moving to the Dallas area. At the end of our little visit, we exchanged telephone numbers and email addresses and agreed to stay in touch with each other better in the future.

I got in the car and began the long drive back to Dallas. I sort of trembled as I drove back thinking about all that had happened in a little more than twenty-four hours. There had been God's voice telling me not to leave Houston and my being led out to where the Emmaus Walk was being held. There were all of the "chance meetings" of a place to stay, and a chance to worship with friends at my former church, and running into biking friends and others. But most of all, it was the conversation with Barbara that had shocked me. I had an incredible fear of hospitals and even had difficulty going to visit someone in a hospital, so I was shocked to think that words came out of my mouth to offer a body part. You just don't do that! And I certainly am not the person to do such a thing. But at least I would not need to do that since Joel would be the one to give her his kidney. Overall, it had just been a very unique and God-filled weekend. And I was looking forward to finally getting home and to studying.

But the events did not end there. The next few weeks I was busy with school and trying to manage life when all of a sudden, I got a call from Barbara. Joel had gone in for some additional tests and they found something that would prevent him from being a donor. I just asked her, "What do I need to do to start the process?"

I had no idea if we would be a match, but the way I figured it was that if we weren't a match, then I would not have to go through with the surgery and giving a kidney. If by some strange coincidence (or God-event) we were a match, then I knew that God would be in it all and it would be OK. Besides, all I could do was think back to that strange weekend and God's voice and all that had happened.

It turned out that we were a perfect match. In fact, I was a much better match than Joel would have been and because of my age it would be easier for me to recover and it would free him up to care for Barbara. We were able to schedule the surgery for spring break, so I did not miss too much school and it was an amazing God-filled time for both of us. Through all of the testing, surgery, and recovery, Barbara and I watched God move in powerful ways. She always said it was a blessing to her to receive the kidney, but it was an even greater blessing to me to be able to give it.

You may be wondering how I felt about committing myself to something that brought up one of my greatest fears. Actually, that was part of the incredible blessing. Through it all God gave me such an amazing peace. I knew without a doubt God was in charge and had been even way back when I sat down in my car and heard the Divine voice saying not to leave Houston. And when I thought about it, it really went back further than that. I could easily trace it back to the decision to go to that seminary and to sign up for that class with Dr. Abraham and traveling back and forth to Houston. And to be honest, if I sat and thought about it, it probably goes back much further than that. God has a way of opening doors and gently guiding us through life . . . if we will only allow the Lord to whisper to us and direct our steps.

Reflection Question:

In what ways are you willing to give of yourself for others?

Divine Encounter 10

Carried by God

How good are you at allowing others to assist you when you need help? I think for a lot of us, we are much more willing to try to give help to others than we are to ask or accept it for ourselves. Yet there are times that we desperately need someone else to step in and lend a hand. Thank goodness for friends who love us and support us and come to our rescue.

That was particularly true during my first year of seminary. For the first time in my life, I was finding myself all alone. My children were both in universities in other cities; my husband was gone; since I had left my career, I no longer saw all of my work colleagues; and because we had moved from Houston, all of my running partners and good friends were a long way away. I did not even have a church family to lean on since we had moved and not found another church in the Dallas area that felt like home. But the one thing I knew was that God was with me and I felt like I was going down the path I was supposed to be traveling . . . to be in seminary and moving toward being a preacher.

I try to be pretty independent and handle things on my own, with God's help of course. However, after giving a kidney, all of a sudden, I realized there was a lot that I could not do. Of course, it would not have mattered had I known before the surgery what all it would involve. It was one of those times when I knew that God was instructing me to obey and help Barbara any way I could. What I discovered was that the surgery is actually more extensive for the one who is giving the kidney than the one receiving it. The incision for the one giving has to be larger to remove the kidney, while the one receiving only has a small incision to place the new organ inside. Of course, the real danger for the one receiving is to make sure that it is a good match and that everything possible is done to make sure that their body does not reject the new kidney at a later stage.

Everything overall went well for both of our surgeries. But after a few days in the hospital, the doctor who performed it wanted both of us to stay in a hotel near the hospital for two more weeks. He just wanted to make sure that if there were any difficulties that we were close to the hospital, especially since neither of us lived in the Houston area. We were down the hall from each other in the hotel and so when we felt like it then we were usually together in one of our rooms visiting and keeping each other company. Barbara's sweet husband, Joel, did a lot of running back and forth and caring for both of us.

However, the time came for me to go back to the Dallas area, and I was discovering all of my limitations. Because of my size, instead of going through the back to get the kidney, they had gone through the front which meant that my incision was from my chest bone all the way down and it had cut through all of my stomach muscles. For that reason, the recovery would last a lot longer. I would not be able to drive for at least six weeks. But there were also some surprises of things that I could no longer do until everything healed. For instance, did you know that you cannot pick up a half-gallon of milk without stomach muscles? It is not an issue that it is painful or that the doctor advises you not to do it, you literally cannot lift things without tightening your stomach muscles to give you that extra strength. I guess I always thought that was just your arm strength, but I was discovering all the ways you use your stomach muscles to move and lift and sit and stand. It was a good reminder of what a magnificent body God has given us humans and how all the parts work together to help us to be active.

I also learned that I could not go up stairs. And once again, it was not just a matter of doctor's orders, which I would have probably ignored and done anyway, but I literally had trouble lifting my feet. My walking was a shuffle at best. I knew I would recover, and I truly had no regrets that I had given the kidney, but I wanted to get back to class and I was afraid I would get behind in my studies. I had thought beforehand that since I was in such great shape that I would have the surgery done over spring break and be back to school the very next week. I had not planned for little challenges like not being able to drive or carry books or go up and down stairs.

When I was being evaluated to see if I could give a kidney in the first place, the entire seminary had been incredibly supportive. They had prayed with me and over me as I went through the different tests and evaluations. And when it was determined that I was a good match and the surgery was scheduled, my seminary friends were there to encourage me. One of my new seminary friends, Patty King, drove me to Houston for the surgery. Then three weeks later after I had been in the hospital as well as the hotel near the hospital for the required time, Patty drove back to Houston to pick me up and take me home to the Dallas area.

Because I was not able to be alone during the recovery time and could not drive to class, the administration at the Perkins School of Theology gave me a dorm room on campus so I could attend classes. I had a wonderful group of friends who knew my class schedule and were glad to meet me at all of the different places so that they could carry my books for me. On one hand, it was incredibly frustrating not to be able to do even little things on my own and having to ask and depend on others for assistance. But on the other hand, it was an unbelievable blessing to have so many different people coming by to assist any way that they possibly could. Some of them were close friends from my classes, some were students or faculty I did not know well who stopped to see what I needed. I felt so much closer to everyone as I was having to depend on them. But I also think it made our entire seminary student body and faculty closer as it seemed to be a joint effort of love and support.

As I think back, I am truly touched by every act of kindness shown to me. One event really demonstrated the love and care of my classmates. I was taking a full load of classes, which were all on the first floor except the Christian Heritage class. It was a fabulous class and Dr. William S. Babcock made it come alive with his stories. I mentioned to two of my friends, Darryl Jordan and Bob Johnson, that I would miss that class. I asked them to pay attention and take good notes so that they could tell me everything. They asked me why I was going to miss class and I explained I could not go up the stairs. They said they would take good notes and started to walk away, but then they stopped, talked for just a moment and came running back. No one should miss Babcock's class! They made a chair with their arms and carried me up the stairs to the classroom. And after class they carried me back down. They were my heroes!

A couple of days later when it was getting close to time for Babcock's class another couple of guys said today was their day to carry me up the stairs. It was wonderful, because I was feeling like such a loser not being able to do anything on my own, and yet the love and support of my classmates made me feel loved.

By the next week the assistant dean had heard about the graciousness of the guys carrying me up to class and though it was considered admirable, they decided they better do something. So, classrooms were moved around, and Dr. Babcock's Christian Heritage class would now meet in the auditorium on the first floor.

I think back on that time and it was not exactly an easy time as I recovered from the surgery. But it was a truly blessed time as people whom even a year before I had not known, rallied around and supported me. Bob and Darryl would always laugh and say I wasn't really that heavy to carry. What they did not totally realize is when they lifted my broken body . . .

they lifted my spirit and gave me the courage to continue on! One of the great ways to see and experience God is through the wonderful individuals that the Lord sends into your life at just the right moment to carry you though the tough times.

Reflection Question:

When have you felt God carrying you?

An Angel's View

I DEFINITELY BELIEVE IN God's perfect timing. I know it doesn't always look so perfect at the time, but often afterward we can look back and see how things worked out much better than what we expected. I also believe that God puts special people in your life for a reason.

Chris Ortegal was one of those special people. She had been our realtor when we moved into our home in Colleyville, but more than that, she had been a good friend. When she had heard that we were having difficulties in our marriage, she came over to check on me. She had been through something similar, and had come through it still a beautiful, vibrant woman. Just watching her gave me hope.

One day we were talking and the topic of World Vision came up. I said I sponsored a child through World Vision, and she shared that on the following Friday there would be a dinner for World Vision, and she thought I ought to go. She said it was $100 per person, and I quickly laughed and said that my days of going to those kinds of events were over. By this time I had left my career, was in seminary, and working hard to make ends meet. She said that she was sitting at a friend's table for the event and was sure she would be glad to have me as her guest. Her friend's name was Anne Holland, and Chris said she was definitely someone I needed to meet. I was grateful for the invitation as Chris encouraged me to mark my calendar and plan on attending the event with her.

Then a few days later the world as we knew it was thrust into a state of shock with the 9/11 attack on the World Trade Center. Even though I was miles away in Texas, it felt as if it were right in my backyard. I know that was true for so many throughout our country. We all watched in horror as the tragic events unfolded in New York, Washington, and Pennsylvania.

With the nation in shock and mourning, I really did not expect the World Vision event to be held that Friday evening. Surprisingly the event was not cancelled but rather became a perfect atmosphere for attendees to join together with a deepened commitment of making our world a better place. The event was held in the back garden of a large mansion in Dallas. I felt honored to be able to join those in attendance. There was a time in my former career where I felt because of my position and my community involvement that I could walk into a black-tie event and be a key player. But that was Houston and this was Dallas, and that was when I had a career instead of being a student. That was also when I felt like a beautiful married woman instead of someone whose husband did not even want her. I have to admit that I felt honored to be there, but I also felt a little out of place.

It had been a busy night. Even though I had not visited with many people, it seemed everyone was busy talking. As the evening ended and Chris and I headed to the car, a beautiful redhead woman came running up. She apologized that she had not had an opportunity to visit with me and said her name was Anne Holland. She asked for my telephone number and said she would try to call me, and we would get together. I gave it to her, but I did not expect a phone call. It was obvious that she was a classy businesswoman. In fact, Chris had mentioned that she owned her own oil company, and sat on the board of World Vision, as well as the Jesus Project. Why in the world would she bother calling me?

The next morning, I was up early and had already finished my run and was busy studying. I was feeling guilty for not staying in the night before to read and study, but I had to admit it had been a glamorous evening and it reminded me of the *good ole days*. About mid-morning I got a phone call and to my surprise it was Anne Holland. She graciously said she was so very sorry we had not had the opportunity to visit last night and asked if I was available for lunch. I said certainly and she named a Mexican food restaurant that was near. We agreed to meet at noon.

Chris had mentioned to Anne what I was going through, and so she asked me to tell her about all that was happening in my life. As I filled in the details, I also took the opportunity to share with her my testimony and why I felt called into the ministry. She shared some of her story with me, and it was amazing to hear all that she had been through and her deep faith in God. We talked nonstop for over two hours, until she had to leave for a commitment. It had been so wonderful to meet her and to talk so deeply. We agreed that we would stay in touch.

I had planned to head home and jump back into my studies, but earlier that morning I had noticed that there was going to be a special televised service at a church near the restaurant. The service was focused on prayer for our country and the victims of 9/11 and would be led by a group of well-known pastors, such as Franklin Graham. I thought what they had to say might be really helpful, so I headed over to the church. I knew I would be a little early but figured I could get a good seat.

I walked into an almost empty sanctuary and started making my way to the front when I looked up and coming in from the other side of the sanctuary was Anne. We saw each other and just laughed. We had not talked about where she was going next and actually, I had not planned to go there, but here we were together again. We took two seats in the middle front and continued our conversation and the sharing of our lives.

It was a really powerful event with inspirational preaching addressing the 9/11 bombings and having faith in God in uncertain times. Afterward, Anne asked if this was the church I normally attended. I said no I had been visiting different churches since we had moved from Houston. She invited me to attend her church—Prestonwood Baptist. I told her I had heard of it, but since I was still learning my way around Dallas I did not know where it was. She suggested that I meet her at her condo the next morning, and we would ride together to church.

Anne's condo was on Turtle Creek, not far from Southern Methodist University where I was going to seminary. She told me the address and said I should just pull up and one of the doormen would park my car and show me in. It was a beautiful area of town, and I arrived at a very impressive building. The doormen greeted me, and one parked my car as the other escorted me to elevators. Anne was on the eighth floor. I went upstairs and walked into her condo, and it was so elegant. The windows were from the floor to the ceiling all the way around allowing for a great view of downtown Dallas in one direction with the Dallas Country Club and SMU in another direction. Her furnishings were stylish and even included a baby grand piano and the artwork was fabulous. She showed me around and everything was exquisite. I told her how beautiful it was and thanked her for inviting me to see it. She stood right there in the middle of the living room and started to take a key off of her key ring and handed it to me. She said that she was going to be gone to Canada for a few weeks, and if I would like to get away from my house for a few days, and be closer to the campus during that time, I was welcome to use it while she was gone. She would let the doormen know that they could expect me and that they would help me with anything I might need.

I stood there in shock. I had just met this woman briefly on Friday evening and we had spent some time visiting yesterday, but she did not really know me that well, and yet she had just handed me the key to her condo and told me I was free to use it. How could anyone be so kind and generous and trusting?

Do you know people like that who just go out of their way to be compassionate? Or maybe that is how you are to other people. God has a way of placing certain people in our path. Sometimes those people are there because we are supposed to love and take care of them, and sometimes it is because we are the ones in need of some tender loving care. God's timing is always perfect when he brings someone into your life. When I think about Chris and Anne, I am particularly touched that they showed up right when I needed them . . . and they showed me a love that could only be from God.

Reflection Question:

When has God sent you angels in a human form?

God Provides

I KNEW THAT WITH our marital situation and leaving my high-paying career we would have to sell our house. But to be honest I was truly dreading that time. We had already moved three times in recent years, and it was difficult enough to do that as a family, but I knew it was going to be incredibly tough to do it on my own. Plus, I was worried about the children. Even though they were both attending college and had their own places to live, they had felt like their real home was wherever Mom and Dad were . . . and that home was changing and would never be the same.

My concern was also the timing of the sale of the house. I was taking a heavy class load in seminary, and I really wanted to just focus on studying. So, my preference was that we sell and move during either the Christmas or summer break so that it would not disrupt classes as much. Actually, I had first thought Christmas would be a better option for when to move. I was going through the evaluation process of whether I would give a kidney or not, and it looked like that would be at spring break if I was a match. Thus, Christmas sounded like a good time to do it and get it over with prior to surgery. We did get a contract for the house around that time, and at first, I was relieved that we could go ahead and get it sold and move. But then in talking with the children, I realized how much of a shock all of this was for them and I felt that we at least needed one more Christmas in this big house before everything was separated and we went our different ways. I was thankful to God when the contract fell through.

The timing for the kidney donation did end up happening near spring break. But then after I had given the kidney, I really started worrying about when the house might sell. Now it was not only the issue of not wanting to miss classes during the semester, but I also knew that there was no way for me to pack and move things until I had more time to recover. Healing from the surgery was definitely going to take longer than I had first anticipated.

I was praying that the sale of the house would not happen until after the spring semester was over.

We made it through most of the semester, but then right before finals we got a contract to sell the house, and it was obvious that this one would go through. With the surgery and classes and trying to manage everything else, I had not had much of an opportunity to look for a place to move. Plus, since I was no longer working in my corporate job and only had a part-time job on campus, I knew I did not have much to spend on a place to live.

When our realtor, Chris Ortegal, and I visited about the upcoming contract, she asked me what my plans were as to where I would move. I cried a little and said I didn't know yet, but I was sure God would provide something. The next few days I was definitely in one of those crying moods. If someone even looked at me wrong, I would start crying. I was going to classes and yet trying to avoid all contact with people. The truth was that I was scared to death of where I was going to end up living.

I had gone to my office on campus to try to get a little work done when I got a call from Anne Holland. Apparently, Chris had mentioned to her that we had a contract on our house. Anne called to say that she owned several properties and maybe one of them would work. She had a couple of houses in the mid-cities area, and she had another condo on Turtle Creek on the twenty-third floor of another building. Or . . . the one she really thought I should consider was the one that she was presently living in.

What? I was shocked to get her phone call in the first place, but especially her suggesting that I move into her condo. She went on to say that she was planning on getting married in the near future, and she would be glad to move out of her beautiful Turtle Creek condo if I would be interested in moving in. She thought it would be a good place for me because it was a great safe area for me to run every morning and as a single woman the doormen would be there to help. It was also really close to the SMU campus.

I was astounded with the offer, but I knew I could not afford it. I told her I really appreciated the offer, but I went on to explain that even if I was still working for the corporation and had my high paying salary, I doubted that I could afford to live in her condo. And certainly, now that I was a struggling student with two children in college and a part-time minimum wage job, there was no way that I could afford to live in her spectacular condo.

That's when she said, "That is what I am trying to tell you—I want to help support your ministry. I'll rent it to you at a low enough price that you can easily afford it."

I was so amazed at Anne's generosity. It was a relief to just find a place to live without having to go out searching for it, but then for it to be this beautiful condo with unbelievable views and in such a wonderful part of town.

But there was something more about Anne's condo that made it special. I could not put my finger on it until I went over and looked at the other condo that she owned a few blocks away. She told me I was welcome to go look at it and then come see her at her home. She would not meet me over at the other location but said that she would call the doormen for that building and they would give me a key to go up to the twenty-third floor to see the condo. I was really excited to go see it since it was even higher up and I figured it had a great view. I picked up the key and went upstairs, but to be honest I did not stay in the condo very long. I glanced out the window and it was in fact a great view, but it just did not feel comfortable. In fact, I realized that as soon as I walked in the building, I had felt uneasy . . . almost like I was not supposed to be there. As I rode the elevator up, my chest started hurting, which was weird since I had been in much taller buildings and had never felt this way. I quickly locked up the condo and headed downstairs to return the key and leave the building. Though everything looked glamorous inside and out, I still had a very uncomfortable feeling that I could not explain.

I hurried over to Anne's condo and I noticed when I walked in that this place had a totally different feel about it. It felt . . . prayed over. We sat down on the couch to visit and she asked me which of the condos I liked best. I told her the other one was lovely, but I really liked this one the best (and I didn't want to mention my strange feelings about the other place). She sighed and said, "Good! There is something about that other building that makes me feel very uncomfortable. That is why I would not meet you over there."

I was both surprised and relieved to hear her say that. I thought I must be imagining things. But she confirmed that she did not know what had happened in that building or what was presently going on, but even though everything looked OK, it still felt sinister. And maybe that is what I loved about her present home; it felt sacred and full of prayers. It felt like it would be a safe place where I could heal and study and serve the Lord.

Anne and Gene were married, and she moved out in perfect time for me to move in. And with regard to God's timing, the closing on our home in Colleyville did not happen until after I was through with finals and could catch my breath in order to handle the move. It was an amazing blessing to be able to move into that glorious condo on the eighth floor on Turtle Creek. God and Anne had provided me a perfect place to call my home for the next year and a half. God is so good!

Reflection Question:

Where have you experienced sacred space?

Divine Encounter 13

Holy Appetizer

OK, SO MOST OF these stories are times where I have seen God move in my own life, but sometimes we need to hear great stories of people with whom I have had the privilege of sharing this life.

I have already told you about Anne Holland and her incredible generosity, but you need to know that she was not just that way to me, she treats everyone with that same kind and generous spirit. Anne fascinates me, a beautiful woman inside as well as out, with her red hair, soft voice, and sparkling laugh. It is obvious that she is one of those individuals who can get things done. But interestingly, she is often working on getting something done for those around her rather than trying to meet her own needs.

I watched Anne at a party at her home one evening and I was impressed with all the different guests who were invited and how she moved among them to make sure that everyone was connected. There was an artist, a former pastor, a taxi driver, a secretary, a socialite, and a variety of others. Diverse nationalities populated the party and all ends of the wealth spectrum. Looking around the room it did not at first appear that anyone there had any connection to anyone else . . . except that they were all good friends of Anne. It was as if she had gone out to collect people and had wanted to bring in a really broad variety of individuals to be part of her . . . blessed treasure.

Yet it was not just that all of these people seemed to come from different backgrounds, but in every case, Anne seemed to quietly be working to help each person who was there. Anne is an incredible listener and when she meets someone, she wants to know his or her story. She listens deeply for what they need and then draws from the other people in her life to help the one that she has just met.

At the party it almost seemed as if she had invited all of these different individuals so that she could find a way to connect them so that they all would mutually benefit each other. She had an innate sense of how to

connect people, beyond what I have ever witnessed. For example, she introduced me to someone who was interested in finding out about how to get a
special telephone number for his business because she knew that I used to
work for Southwestern Bell. And because I was getting ready to move, she
introduced me to a gentleman who owned a shipping company and might
be able to use one of his trucks to help transport my belongings. It was random things that united people, but it was obvious that Anne was the type of
person who noticed a need and then did everything she possibly could to
meet it. I think sometimes the person she was helping may not have even
fully realized what types of things might be a benefit for them. And yet Anne
seemed to be able to analyze the situation and creatively imagine how some
skill or talent or resource that someone else possessed might be of use if she
could bring the two individuals together. Yet though she had this instinctive
ability to recognize possible solutions, it seemed as if her focus was for the
betterment of others and how to benefit those around her rather than to
look to her own needs. She has this virtue of generosity and networking with
creative caring that I have very seldom witnessed.

Among all the different people Anne introduced me to, there is one
person that I will never forget. Her name was Anna Marie. Anna Marie had
grown up in Italy and had some powerful stories to tell about her childhood
and all that she had been through in life. Though she had faced challenges
that most people could not even imagine, she had this joy and excitement
about life. Every day was a new day and an opportunity to discover something exciting. One of my favorite stories happened not long after she had
come to the United States.

A friend had set Anna Marie up on a blind date. She had been told that
he was a really nice guy. They had gone out to eat on Saturday evening and
had a lot of fun. He told her that he was a cantor at a Church of Christ and
asked if she would like to go to church with him the following day. She had
never been to a Church of Christ, but she had been in a Catholic orphanage
for a short time when she was young, so she decided that she would go with
him. He had told her that they would have lunch after church.

When they went into church, he explained he would need to sit on
the chancel to lead the music and he wanted her to sit on the very front
row so that she would be close. After a while, it seemed to Anna Marie that
the service was going on for a long time and she was starting to get hungry
since she had not had a chance to eat breakfast. She was looking forward to
lunch and was not really paying that much attention to what was going on
in the service. Then all of a sudden, a man showed up with a gold tray and a
giant cracker on the tray. He stood right beside her as if he was wanting her

to take it. So naturally, she thought, "How nice, they are serving appetizers since this service is going on for so long."

She reached over and took the big cracker. She looked at it and decided that it was really too big for her to sit there and eat in one setting, so she broke it in half and put half of it in her purse for later and started munching on the other half that was still in her hand. Then she realized that the man was still standing there with his gold tray and she decided he must be waiting for a tip. She glanced up at him and he said, "Miss, if you don't mind, may I have the half of the holy bread that you placed in your purse so that I can serve Holy Communion to the rest of the congregation?"

How embarrassing! She had no idea that they would serve Holy Communion like that! The little bit of time that she had been at the Catholic orphanage, it was done very differently.

Anna Marie laughs as she tells the story. It was an experience that was completely foreign to anything she had done before. But that is not the end of the story. A few minutes later the gentleman returned with a little gold tray full of tiny little cups of juice. When he offered it to her, he said, "Miss, if you don't mind, please just take one."

Don't you love it that we are all different and our lives are made up of diverse experiences that help us each to have our unique perspectives? I think God uses those individuals who look at life from a different point of view than our own in order to expand our world and help us to recognize that life does not always look exactly the same for all of us. Maybe that is the great thing about collecting people from a variety of walks of life—it is a chance to see things from a delightfully new perspective.

Reflection Question:

When has God helped you see things from a different perspective?

Divine Encounter 14

The Power of Hospitality

As I WAS BECOMING oriented in my new life at the seminary, I discovered I had not yet found a church that I felt comfortable with since I had moved from Houston. I remember lamenting about this conundrum with one of my professors only to be surprised at his response. He pointed out that might not be such a bad thing for right now. He told me I should take advantage of the fact that I was not presently serving or actively involved in a particular church at this time. Instead, I should continue to visit different ones. He said it would be a good chance to notice the various distinctions that each of the churches had to offer. It would give me the opportunity to discover the church which best aligns with my needs and desires. And it would also be insightful for what things seemed to work best and felt the most welcoming. I could then remember and incorporate those distinctions where I served as pastor.

So . . . I visited lots and lots of churches, every Sunday morning, and sometimes I would squeeze in two different church services on a Sunday. It really was a good way to see how the music was done, the order of service, how guests were welcomed, and even the hospitality before and after the services. There is a multitude of churches in Dallas, so there was no shortage of different ones to attend.

I remembered meeting Dr. Stan Copeland at a meeting with my former pastor from Houston about a year before. I decided I would like to hear him preach and so I went to Lovers Lane United Methodist Church. It is a huge, beautiful church which looks like a stained glass box. It doesn't just have stained glass windows; literally, the walls are stained glass. Where some churches may have lots of stained glass windows that tell the biblical story, at Lovers Lane the walls are all glass and a splash of color starts at the bottom back and sweeps all the way along the sides of the long sanctuary until the colors meet up high behind the chancel area. Especially on a sunny day, you feel like you are inside a beautiful, sacred, jeweled box. It is truly magnificent.

That first Sunday morning I walked nervously up to the church. As I got closer, the door was swung open and a wonderful older gentleman greeted me. His nametag said that he was Raymond Hayes and he acted so delighted to see me. He made me feel extremely welcomed and asked me what my name was. I told him Keva and he said, "Well, Keva, welcome to Lovers Lane." I also met another gentleman inside and his name was Frank Jackson and he also was very gracious and welcoming. I took a seat in the sanctuary and it was a wonderful service. Both Dr. Copeland's sermon and the music were excellent, and it just all felt comfortable. I thought if I was not in the process of trying to visit different churches that this might be one that I would attend again.

The next few weeks I continued to visit other churches and to take notes about the things that seemed to work and what didn't seem as good. One Sunday morning, four weeks later, I had planned to visit another church; but as I was driving, I decided to go back to Lovers Lane. Something about it had felt sacred, loving, and welcoming when I had attended before, and that particular morning I was not in the mood to attend a new church where I might be ignored. Unfortunately, I had visited several of those types of churches where no one ever greeted or acknowledged me, and it left me feeling so incredibly lonely. Those were the churches where the members were all glad to see each other and were so busy talking to the people that they know that the guests were ignored. I thought at least one of those nice gentlemen who were greeters at Lovers Lane would make me feel welcomed.

Sure enough, as I walked up to the entry of Lovers Lane, once again Raymond Hayes threw open the door to greet me. Not only did he welcome me with a big smile, but he called me by name. "Keva, so glad you are back. I missed you."

Oh, my goodness, this man remembered my name from several weeks ago. My name! And he pronounced it correctly. It is an unusual name, but Dale Carnegie is right—there is nothing sweeter than to hear someone call you by name. Frank was also there to welcome me and make me feel special. Have you ever been touched deeply just because someone greeted you or called you by name?

Now I'm sure Dr. Copeland's message was once again excellent and I'm sure the choir and organ music and everything else was done extremely well, but the biggest impact for me was the hospitality that an older gentleman showed me as he opened the door for me. Not long afterward, I became a member of Lovers Lane. There were lots of great programs and activities going on there, but the biggest draw for me was two ushers who went out of their way to make me feel welcome and special.

That greeting not only brought me to that church, but it impacted my life in other ways. After I had attended there for a little while, Dr. Stan Copeland and I got to know each other a little better. One Sunday after the service he asked if I might consider working part-time at the church. I could not because my scholarship for seminary was tied to the fact I was working part-time for the school. But later, when I was in a better position, I jumped at the chance to join the staff of Lovers Lane.

It was such an incredible learning experience to serve under Stan Copeland and work with David McLarin, Tom Hudspeth, Donna Whitehead, and other staff members. Plus, I fell in love with the congregation. I have many longtime friends from there. It was such a blessing to serve there and to learn how to be in ministry. When I look back, I remember it all started with two ushers who loved the Lord and helped everyone who walked in the door feel that love. I saw God in how they extended that holy invitation to be a part of something special. We each have a chance to open our eyes and see God moving around us in the people who are in our lives. And we also have a chance to demonstrate God's love when we go out of our way to greet and welcome others.

Reflection Question:

When have you seen God through other people?

Divine Encounter 15

God Knows Our Needs

ANNE HAD BEEN so gracious to allow me to live for a year and a half in her beautiful condo on Turtle Creek. However, I still had another year and a half before I finished seminary. She said I could continue to stay there, but I was feeling guilty about living there. I knew she could sell it for a tremendous price or even if she rented it for what it really should be bringing in, it would be much, much more than what she was getting from me. She was a good friend and I did not want to take advantage of her generosity, so over the Christmas holidays I started looking for somewhere else to live.

With the cost of my children's tuition, my tuition, and helping with all our living expenses, there was simply not a lot of money to spare. By this time, I was on the staff at Lovers Lane United Methodist Church as a part-time local student pastor. The pay was a little better than working part-time on the campus. But I was nervous about finding a new place to live that I could afford.

My son, Kevin, came home for the Christmas holidays and together we started searching for my next home. He really wanted us to get a two-bedroom place so he would have his own room. I tried to explain that normally he was off at his university so it would be more cost effective if I just had a one-bedroom. But I realized that from his point of view, wherever I moved was really his home where he would come back to during the holidays and summer vacation. It would be where he would leave a lot of his belongings, and that place needed to feel like it was also his. My daughter, LeeRand, who is older, was busy with her life in Houston and so it was not the same for her. Yet it was obviously important for Kevin to feel like he had a home.

We continued to look at apartments or duplexes or anything that looked like a possibility of some place that I could afford and still attend seminary. Nothing met the criteria or felt like it was where I was supposed to be living. I was getting a little worried, but I remembered that last time God had provided beyond what I could ever imagine so I trusted God would do the same now. We found a couple of possibilities. They were not perfect, and the price was a little higher than my comfort level, but perhaps I could do it. The one I was finally going to try to rent was very small, but at least the building was in a good area. It was more than I could afford, but my prayer was that if I watched my budget closely and absolutely did not spend anything extra, I could somehow manage to pay my rent and survive. Before I finalized the deal, I received a call from Linda Vorhies, one of the members of Lovers Lane United Methodist Church. I had gotten to know Linda that past summer when we had gone on a mission trip to Tegucigalpa, Honduras. She was so much fun!

Linda's parents had a huge house on Beverly Drive not far from SMU. Her father had passed away a while back, but her mother had just died about three years before. Since her mother had designed the house and her father had built it, and it was full of their furniture, artwork, and things from all over the world, Linda had not wanted to sell it. She wanted someone to live there and make sure things were safe. She offered to let me live there for free while I attended seminary and worked on staff at Lovers Lane UMC. It was an incredible opportunity because it was a really large home with a swimming pool and guesthouse. It was in the Highland Park / Beverly Drive area of Dallas and if you are familiar with that neighborhood, you are aware of the many mansions and spectacular homes in that area. The home was fully furnished with beautiful furniture and art pieces from Linda's parents' world travels. There were plenty of bedrooms (I think there were six not counting the guest house) so Kevin was able to have his own whenever he came home from school. And it was a great place for me.

Linda's generosity was such an amazing blessing in my life. Once again, I felt God had provided for me not only by putting the right person in my life to help me while I was in seminary, but also God gave me a wonderful, safe home.

I am constantly astounded by how God blesses us beyond our imaginations. I think the Lord has a way of signaling to our soul when something feels right or when we are supposed to keep looking and not just settle for second best. We might think we do not deserve anything but the minimal resources, yet God wants to surprise us with extravagant blessings, not because we did anything special, but because *the Lord* is special and wants to shower us with amazing love.

Reflection Question:

When has God provided for you well beyond your expectations?

Divine Encounter 16

Seeing the Face of God

I'M NOT SURE WHEN or why I developed a fear of hospitals, but it was definitely real. I know I had kidney problems when I was an infant and toddler. I'm not sure what all of the issues were, but I was in the hospital during my early years and had minor surgery. My mother would tell the story about my fear of doctors and that I knew they were the ones who wore white coats. The moment someone with a white coat opened the door of the hospital room or the examining room, I would start screaming. They finally realized that it was the "white coat" that gave away their identity and so as long as they left it outside of the room then I was a little calmer.

I was so fearful of men in white coats that I even made a scene at the local Piggly Wiggly Grocery Store. My mother had taken me to the grocery store with her and I was riding in the cart. When we came near the meat counter, I happened to see the butcher with his white coat on. My mother said that I stood up in the grocery cart and screamed at the top of my lungs, "You can't take off my panties, you can't take off my panties, you can't take off my panties." Poor guy—I think it was as traumatic for him as it was for me.

You would think that you could outgrow childhood fears and I did in some respects. I was finally better about going to see a doctor, but still very uncomfortable if I had to go into a hospital for any reason. Just walking into a hospital would either make me nauseated or cause me to have a panic attack.

One of the most embarrassing times was right after I had started working for Southwestern Bell Telephone. I managed a crew of technicians. One of them had gotten sick or hurt while she was off for lunch. I received a call from the hospital where she was. In turn, I called my boss to let him know what was going on and to ask what needed to be done. He explained there was a certain form which needed to be completed. I would have to go to the hospital, check on her, and get the information. I suggested I could just call the hospital and talk with her to find out all the information. He made it very clear, that as part of my job as a supervisor, I should personally go to the hospital.

I had been told she was in the Emergency Room, so I had parked in the front of the hospital. I walked in the main doors and asked where the Emergency Room was. Immediately, I started having a panic attack and passed out. They thought there was something seriously wrong with me, and so I was quickly transferred to the Emergency Room. When I woke up, I was desperately trying to tell them that the only thing I needed was to get out of the hospital. Needless to say, I did not get the form filled out.

All that to say, I had a big fear of hospitals! Over the years there were various times that I had to be in the hospital—two babies, two back surgeries, and a few other instances. None of them were easy. The only exception was when I gave the kidney and that time, I had an incredible sense that God had orchestrated it all, and so I was more comfortable with the whole situation. (Divine Encounter 9, "Sharing a Part of Me," gives the details of how God moved in that situation, and why that particular surgery/hospital stay was not as frightening.) Yet for the most part, I would get extremely nervous about going to visit anyone in the hospital and would avoid it at all cost.

When I served at Lovers Lane United Methodist Church there were about ten associate pastors, and so we rotated hospital visits. I was successful for a while of getting someone else to cover my days. However, Rev. Dudley Dancer, who was over our pastoral care, figured out what was going on. He was a wonderfully kind, compassionate pastor, so he tried to help me get over the fear.

I realized my third year of seminary that being a minister in the local church definitely included doing hospital visits. To be honest, I loved the idea of being a preacher, but if I could pick and choose job responsibilities, then the two that I would leave out would be hospital visits and funerals. Both of those responsibilities seemed incredibly difficult and it made me start doubting whether I could really become a pastor.

I tried to imagine how I could handle being a pastor if I was afraid to visit people at the hospital. I guessed I could call on the phone to someone who was about to go into surgery, and I could tell them that if they could somehow make it over to the window that they could see me wave to them from the parking lot. "By the way, I won't come in to pray for you (because I am too frightened to walk in the building), but don't you worry a bit. I'm sure you will be just fine, and I'll be out here praying." Somehow, I did not think that would work.

Before my final year of seminary, I knew I had to determine if I could go into hospitals. If not, then I figured that I would have to go for my PhD and just teach homiletics instead of actually preach. I had to find a way to get over my fear of hospitals and if I couldn't, then I needed to start making plans to go a different direction in ministry.

I decided I would apply for a CPE (Clinical Pastoral Education) or in other words, a chaplaincy at a hospital. I was going to do it the summer between my third and fourth seminary years, and my hope was that I would be able to stick with it the entire summer and come out stronger by doing it. If so, I could move forward in becoming a local church pastor. And if not, then I would have to adjust my long-term goals. I really felt that God had called me to preach and so I was going to do everything I possibly could to follow through with that plan.

I had applied at three different hospitals and was offered a position in all three of them, but the one I thought might be easier to handle was Children's Medical Center. The walls were brightly painted, and it did not smell like a hospital, so maybe it would be an easier atmosphere in which to adjust. However, the part that I did not really think about was how difficult it would be to watch young children going through such devastating illnesses and trauma.

Every morning was a huge effort just to get to the hospital. I would wake up and already be dreading going there and would make myself sick just thinking about it. I would drive to the hospital, nauseated and scared. Then I would sit in my car praying and telling myself that I could do this! I would watch as others would pull into the parking garage and jump out of their cars and walk in like it was no big deal, and I would tell myself that if they could go in there that I could do it too.

There were ten of us doing a CPE at Children's that summer. It was a great group and very supportive. It also was very obvious that the rest of them felt much more comfortable in this environment than I did. We would normally meet in the CPE lounge early each morning to do a devotional, get our instructions for the day, and then head out to our various areas of responsibilities. I was assigned to both the Emergency Room and the fifth floor, which was for patients dealing with kidney and liver issues.

One morning I was feeling particularly vulnerable. I had been sick with my nerves and cried most of the morning. I just could not motivate myself to walk into the rooms of these precious children where some of them were struggling and having such a difficult time. My heart broke for them, as well as for their loving parents who often watched helplessly. If I went to see someone, I wanted to be a benefit and a support to them, yet the way I was feeling, how could I be of any help? I was really close to walking into the director's office and admitting that I needed to quit. Instead I went to the chapel to pray that I might hear from God and have the courage to do what needed to be done.

The chapel at Children's Medical has seating on a couple of sides and there are some columns in the middle of the room with an altar on the far side. It is actually possible to sit behind one of the columns so that someone glancing in would not know others were in the chapel. I had come in to pray, but to be honest, . . . I had also come to hide, and so I was sitting behind the column.

Sitting there quietly I heard the door open. It sounded like it was a father and a young child. I felt like I was eavesdropping as I listened to their conversation. The father explained this was a special place where people could come and pray to God, and they would pray before they went home. It sounded like they had sat down together, and the father was instructing the child to bow their head and fold their hands and repeat after him. The father led the child through this heartfelt prayer to thank God they were OK and would be able to go home. They asked God to be with all of the other boys and girls and to make them well so they too could go home. Then they both said amen. It was a sweet and simple prayer and as the father said a few words then the small child would repeat them in their innocent little voice.

It was one of the most touching things I had ever heard. And as I sat there on the other side of the column, I desperately wanted to look around it and see the precious child. I had no idea if it was a little girl or a little boy and I could not particularly hear anything in the accent to tell me what nationality they were and I had no idea how old the child was, though they sounded fairly young. It sounded like they were leaving, and I knew if they walked out, I would never have my questions answered as to who this child was, but at the same time I did not want to make it known that I had been sitting there listening to their intimate conversation with God. I was sitting there staring at the column wishing I had x-ray vision and could get a glance at them before they left, when all of a sudden . . . this little face popped around the column and smiled at me. It was the most beautiful child ever with a face that glowed and eyes that sort of sparkled and it was as if they were saying, "Hi! I knew you were back there. Love you!" Though they really did not say anything; that is just what I imagined that smile and the sparkling eyes were communicating. Afterward, I realized that I still could not tell you if it was a boy or a girl or the nationality or the age—all I could remember were the eyes and the smile and it felt like I had gotten a glimpse of God in that moment, or maybe one of God's little angels.

Once again it felt like one of those moments when God was saying, "It is OK, I'm right here with you." That was exactly what I needed to inspire me to go on with my hospital rounds and visit more of God's little angels. At that time, I still struggled with my fear, but I knew that God was with me, and so it gave me the courage to face that fear recognizing that I was not doing it on my own.

Reflection Question:

When has God calmed your fear?

Divine Encounter 17

Why Me, Lord?

Working at Children's Medical Center was not an easy assignment for me, but it certainly was an educational one. Any time that you put yourself in a situation that is beyond your comfort zone you are bound to grow. Also, just being in an environment that was different than what I was used to doing in the business world opened my eyes to all that needs to be done in a hospital and particularly in caring for not only the physical health of patients, but also the mental, emotional, and spiritual health of all involved. I saw doctors and nurses and hospital staff working incredibly hard to make a difference in the lives of these precious children, as well as their parents, their siblings, and the extended families. Everyone seemed to carry an extra sensitivity to the struggles that others were going through.

It was such an honor to be doing a CPE at that hospital and to have the chance to be a chaplain and walk beside this brave group of individuals. I had the privilege to listen to and support the medical team and to pray with the parents and to love and encourage the children. It was easy to get close to a family as I supported them, and there were times when that was a real blessing as I saw things improve and the child get healthier and able to leave. And even though it was sometimes tough to say goodbye, I was always excited that they were given the opportunity to go home.

But there were also those times when things did not go well and in the end the family would leave the hospital and go home, but only after having to say a final goodbye to their adorable child. Let's face it, I was not good with illness or death and so I worried whether I had what was needed to support these families as they went through the most difficult times of their lives. Someone else would be better at this, someone else would have the ability to not be overwhelmed with emotions, someone else would have more compassion and wisdom, and someone else would know the right words to say during those times when I was completely speechless. I felt like all I could do was cry along with them and that did not seem to be very supportive. Sometimes it seemed like more than I could handle.

I recently came across something I had written as I was working the night shift following a particularly difficult day:

> Lord, it is more than I can handle . . .
>
> > It is more than I can handle to watch children suffering and parents crying.
> >
> > It is more than I can handle to stand on the sidelines and watch helplessly.
> >
> > It is more than I can handle to see a baby dying.
>
> Lord, I have so many questions . . .
>
> > Why is there such pain surrounding these precious innocents?
> >
> > What could these virtuous souls have done to deserve this?
> >
> > Does all of this anguish really make sense?
>
> Lord, why did you put me here . . .
>
> > Is there a reason that I have been asked to serve in this capacity?
> >
> > A summer wrapped in witnessing other's pain.
> >
> > I liked the world better when I was surrounded with all that was pretty.
>
> Lord, don't leave me by myself . . .
>
> > I know there is a purpose for my summer CPE.
> >
> > And I will try to stick it out until the very end,
> >
> > But please, Lord, always stay right beside me.

One of the questions I would often ask myself as I struggled with this assignment was, "Why me, Lord? What am I doing here?" I did not feel qualified to help, and I worried about hurting others by my not knowing what to say or do. As a pastor I knew that sometimes people say things that they think will be helpful, and yet it ends up being painful to the individual they were attempting to reassure. I did not want to say the wrong thing during those critical times. You want to be encouraging, but if there is no hope, am I giving a parent false hope so that later on it becomes even more devastating? On the other hand, as a chaplain and a representative of God, I have to be the one who reminds them they can trust in the Lord and that he is bigger than anything else. I just desperately wanted wisdom for the right words at those difficult times so that I could lead them lovingly in the direction that they needed to go and bring them closer to the Lord to help them in the long term. I struggled with whether I was the right person for this position, and so I continued to ask, "Why me, Lord?"

And then one day I heard that same question asked, but it was asked in a different way than I had ever imagined, and it changed something inside me. You would think that those who were suffering the most would be the ones to ask the question, "Why me, Lord?" I was on the Oncology ward that served young cancer patients, one of the most challenging units for me emotionally. Many of the children had been there for long durations of time while others came in and out of the hospital many times. That meant that their families had been there with them. There is something deeply touching about watching various families of patients. They hurt for their own child and their family struggles, but they are also extra sensitive to the pain that others are going through. Because of that, they seem to have an enhanced sense of how to support each other and what will make a difference to another parent in a room down the hall.

Many had been in the hospital with their child so much that they had passed each other in the hall and ridden the elevator together and sat in the waiting room at the same time and so they knew each other's stories. They compared notes about treatments and favorite nurses and the food in the cafeteria. So, they bonded. And they were battling the same war even if it was from different points of view; they were all fighting for their children's lives and health.

I guess that is why one day when I was called upstairs to support a family whose child was near death, I noticed some of the parents of other patients gathered in the hall praying. They could sense that death was on the floor and was near one who was dear to all of them. I supported the family through that difficult passing by being there for them and praying over their child and their family. Then after the precious child had breathed their last breath and I helped the parents to say their final goodbye, I had remained in the room to help do some of the finishing responsibilities with the nurses. A little later I happened to walk down the hall, and I saw the mother of one of the other patients sitting in the waiting room weeping. At first, I worried and thought something had happened to her child. I went in to visit with her and comfort her. All she could say was, "Why me, Lord? Why me?" That just confirmed my worst fear, something must have happened to her child. I thought, "Oh Lord, please not two children and two families devastated in the same afternoon! Please, Lord!" Yet when she finally calmed down, I realized that her child was sleeping soundly in her room and was improving.

The "Why me, Lord?" was not a cry lamenting the struggles that she and her family were going through, actually it was just the opposite. She was having difficulty understanding "Why am I so blessed that I get to keep my child for now and my friend has lost hers? Why me, Lord?" She knew that she did not love her child more than the other mother, and her child was not more precious than the one that had passed away, yet death had not come to their door. It was in that moment that I saw God in such a powerful way, and I realized that personally I have so very much for which to be thankful.

You know, often the things that we complain and whine about are really not that big if we would just look around and see what difficulties others are struggling with. So maybe instead of feeling sorry for ourselves and whimpering, "Why me, Lord? Why did things not go the way I wanted?" we need to count our blessings and say, "Why me, Lord? Why have you chosen to bless me in so many ways?"

Reflection Question:

Where do you recognize God's blessings in your life?

Divine Encounter 18

It Is Not about Me

WHEN I DECIDED TO do my CPE at Children's Medical, I somehow envisioned being a chaplain to children would be easier than dealing with health issues for adults. I guess I did not really think that all the way through. It is incredibly tough to watch a small child cry and suffer through something painful. And since I was assigned to the Emergency Room, I realized that a lot of what I was doing was trying to work with parents who were frantic about their child. Yet here I was still struggling to deal with my own fear of working in the hospital while at the same time attempting to be a calming spirit to others. Sometimes I wondered if people were able to sense my underlying anxiety and that I often felt emotionally overwhelmed. Was I helping or hurting in a crisis situation? I was trying desperately to put on a good front and encourage all who were involved that everything was going to be just fine. I knew if I could remain calm and be a tranquil presence, even in the midst of chaos and tragedy, it would help bring their emotional level a little lower so they could better handle what was going on for their child. When you are panicked and highly emotional it just causes the entire situation to be even more stressful for all involved. It was critical that I try to be a positive peaceful influence during these tough situations.

Since I was part of the Emergency Room team, I was given a pager. If a crisis situation came up, then everyone on our team, including trauma doctors and nurses and the various specialists, were paged and we were all to report to the ambulance dock. There were probably a dozen of us on the Emergency Team. My role was to handle the parents. If a child was ill or injured and it was a crisis situation, then the rest of the team would quickly take the child into the trauma room and begin evaluating them and deciding what course of action needed to be taken. That was not the time when the parents needed to be in there upset about what was going on. So officially, I was supposed to grab the parents and gather all the information I could about what had happened, while also calming them down and trying to support them. Under no circumstances was I to allow a parent to go into the trauma room. Especially when doctors and nurses were trying to move fast to handle a critical situation, they did not need the parent in the middle of the evaluation and the medical crisis. Also, it can be overwhelming for a parent to see their precious child in such a perilous state. It is always much better to try to calm the situation down in order to evaluate the best and quickest strategy for a medical emergency.

I will always remember a particular time when we got the page that an ambulance was en route to our hospital. As per protocol, the team all gathered in the hall right outside the ambulance door and the leader of the team began filling us in on the details they had at that time. Apparently, a father had been driving his daughter and two other girls on a summer trip. There was a wreck and all in the car had varying levels of injuries. The wreck had occurred about one hundred miles from Dallas, so the father and one of the girls, who only had slight injuries, were taken to a local hospital, but the other two girls had been life flighted to Dallas. One of the girls was twelve years old, so she would be coming to our hospital. The other child was thirteen years old. Although she would be coming into the same ambulance dock, she would go next door to Parkland, the huge county hospital.

The girls arrived and were quickly transported to the appropriate trauma rooms. We were given the names of the girls and the father who had been involved in the wreck. I knew that frantic parents would be arriving soon. Sure enough, they arrived. The first one who came in was a beautiful young woman who said that it had been her ex-husband driving the car. She had heard that he and their daughter were at the local hospital with minor injuries, but she had shown up at Children's Medical because she was told that the other two girls would be coming to this hospital. She wanted to be there to support them. She asked how the girls were and all I could say was that it was still too early to know anything yet since the ambulance had just arrived.

About that time a couple entered the ER, and they were obviously parents of one of the girls. I introduced myself and realized that it was their daughter in our trauma room. I tried to calm them, but they were both beside themselves with worry and fear. When the husband realized that his daughter was in the room right behind us, he decided he was going in there. I tried to stop him, but he almost knocked me down trying to go in. I managed to keep the mothers outside and tried to explain that we needed to give the doctors a chance to evaluate the situation and do whatever needed to be done to help the young girl. The mother who had arrived first was lovingly trying to comfort her friend as the distraught mother worried about her daughter in the trauma room.

In a moment the husband came back into the waiting room, his face pale. His wife quickly started asking him how their daughter was. At first all he could say was that there was a lot of blood, a whole lot of blood, it was tough to tell. But then he said, "That is not our daughter." I watched as the first mother's face went white and she asked who it was that was in there. He looked at her compassionately and said, "I really don't know, I couldn't tell, but whoever it is she has a cheerleading ring on." The mother sort of caught herself and said that could be either her daughter or the other little girl.

I realized that we had a problem because we were not sure which girl was at each of the hospitals. I had a feeling that the couple's daughter was next door at Parkland, so I grabbed an intern and asked him to walk them over to that Emergency Room. But it also meant that I needed to take this mother into the trauma room to see if that was her daughter or the daughter of the family that was still on their way to the hospital. I slipped into the trauma room and quickly explained the situation to the doctors and asked them to hold off for just a moment and cover what they needed to so that the mother might come in to identify her daughter. They did the best they could, and I brought the mother in. She took one look at the girl's feet and recognized them as her daughter's. This was Alexia. We went back out of the room.

My heart broke for this sweet woman who had thought at first that her child was not badly hurt and had come just to support her friends. And then all of a sudden, discovered that it was her precious daughter in that room fighting for her life. The last girl's family arrived and came rushing in thinking that their child was seriously injured. And then it was explained that apparently, she was the one who was only slightly injured and was being taken care of at the local hospital a distance away. I watched as fear turned into joy and relief and then into sorrow and compassion for their friend who was now dealing with what they had thought would be their nightmare. They left to go find and take care of their own child. And I sat with this brokenhearted mother who was in shock over what she had just realized.

Alexia needed emergency surgery and then was sent to ICU. I sat with this sweet mother as much as I possibly could. We had bonded in those traumatic moments when she first discovered that it was her daughter who was fighting for her life. I would quickly handle some of my other responsibilities and then hurry back to be by her side as she prayed that her daughter would wake up from this nightmare. Other family and friends came to check on the young girl, but her mother never left her side, other than when Alexia was in surgery.

By the third day the doctors were concerned that Alexia might be brain dead and only being kept alive by the machines. They needed to talk with the parents about what would be happening, and they asked me to be a part of those conversations. By this time, the girl's father had been released from the other hospital and was in the waiting room. We gathered in a small conference room, and I prayed before we began the discussion. Then the doctor explained his concerns and talked about what would need to be done to test to see if there was any brain activity. It definitely was not an easy conversation for anyone. The parents agreed and things were set up to do the testing. The mother was firm that she wanted to remain in the room with her daughter throughout all of the testing. In the end, the results were not good. Alexia was brain dead and it was the machines keeping her heart beating and oxygen flowing through her lungs. Even though we all deep down knew that Alexia's body probably could not have recovered from such a trauma, I think we were holding on to a tiny glimmer of hope until those tests were completed. Now it was evident that there was nothing else that could be done.

The next part was my responsibility as a chaplain. I needed to sit down with the parents to see if they might be willing to donate their child's organs in order to save other lives. It was one of the most difficult things I have ever done, to have to say, "I am so very sorry about the loss of your precious daughter, but would you consider donating her organs so that someone else might live?" I certainly knew the value of organ donation and that it could save lives. (One organ donor can save up to eight lives and that same donor can also save or improve the lives of up to fifty people by donating tissues and eyes.) However, it is one thing to be the one benefitting from an organ donation, quite another to be the family that is letting go of a loved one. But as I visited with them, both Alexia's mother and father agreed that she had always been a loving child who would do anything for others so they truly felt that she would want her organs donated to help others.

I was relieved that they were so gracious to make the donation and I knew it would make a big difference, but then Alexia's mother made one other request. She stated that she had not left her daughter's side since she came into the hospital and she did not want to leave her until her heart stopped beating, so she said that she wanted to be in the operating room when her organs were harvested. I panicked because I did not want them to change their minds about donating the organs, but I also had grown close to this mother and I knew that while she needed this for closure, it would not be a possibility.

I explained that there was no way that, as a parent, she could be in the operating room while they were harvesting Alexia's organs, nor did I think that would be a good thing for her emotionally to have as her last memory of her daughter. But then additional words came out of my mouth, and I don't know where they came from. In the urgency and heartbreak of the moment I told her she could not go in the operating room as a parent, but if she wanted, I would go in there and be with Alexia throughout the surgery for her. I saw relief come over this mother's face as she agreed that if I would be in the operating room with Alexia then she would sign the paperwork to donate her daughter's organs.

I was relieved to hear she would go forward with the organ donation. But then I thought, "Oh my goodness! What have I just done?" I had committed to this loving mother that I would do something I was not sure I was capable of doing. After all, I was the one who was sick every morning just knowing I would have to walk into the hospital. And I was the one who sat in my car and prayed for a long time before actually coming in the building and then in the afternoons would get in my car and cry before I could drive home. How in the world could I go into an operating room?

But I had made a commitment to this loving mother, this woman I had spent hours sitting beside for the last three days, this friend. And I planned to do everything I possibly could to uphold the trust she had put in me.

The surgery to harvest the organs was scheduled for the following morning. I was really supposed to be off, but I knew I would be there. I had gotten there early so I could scrub and suit up for the operating room. A surgical nurse guided me through everything and then pointed me to the right operating room. When I went in, the room was basically empty except for two people on the far side of the room. They were busy counting and recounting everything to make sure it was all set for the harvesting and distributing the organs to different places. I stood over in a corner where I was out of the way and I just watched while wishing I was anywhere in the world except there.

The more I kept thinking about it, the more I started to panic. What was I doing here? Why in the world did I commit to do this? What if I threw up during the surgery or passed out or somehow messed up everything? Others were desperate for these organs and I could possibly destroy their chances by being in this room. How dare I tell that mother I would do this! I can't do it. Lord, get me out of here!

I looked over toward the door that I had come through and it looked like it was about a mile away. I needed to get all the way to the door and if I could get it open, then I knew the sinks were on the other side. My plan was to crawl under the sink and hide. I had to get out of this room! I started walking over toward the door, and the closer I got the more I realized I was about to pass out. My vision became darkness closing in like two sliding doors getting narrower and narrower. I had to get out of the operating room before I fainted. I noticed that there was a straight back chair over by the door. I did not make it to the door, but I did make it to the chair, and so I tried to calmly sit down and pretend that everything was just fine. I could not see anything, but I kept telling myself to breath and not fall out of the chair. I knew if I could rest for a moment that the fainting feeling would pass.

I had the surgical cap and mask on, so I was hoping that those in the room could not tell that I was not feeling that well. I sat there for a moment and I could feel my heart rate beginning to slow down and my sight was starting to come back. I kept telling myself to breath, sit up tall, and do not fall out of the chair.

As my eyesight got better, I noticed that one of the surgical nurses across the room was looking at me. I was hoping that she could not tell that my eyes were dilated or my forehead sweating. She started walking toward me, and I figured I was about to be escorted out of the room and I would not be able to fulfill my promise to Alexia's mother. But instead of coming over and facing me, she came and stood beside me, and she thanked me for being there. She went on to explain that they had never had a chaplain bother to come into the operating room before; it was as if chaplains did not realize how difficult this was on the medical staff. She went on to explain that this was the same operating team that had done Alexia's emergency surgery a couple of days ago in an effort to save her life. Now they would have to harvest her organs.

As she talked, I realized several important things. First, I had originally thought that I was at that hospital to minister to the children. Slowly, I realized that it meant also ministering to the parents. But somewhere in all of that, I had neglected the fact that the doctors and nurses and the other medical staff are all intimately connected in every case. They need love and support as well. I started talking to her about how important her job was and that she was making a big difference in other lives. And even though it was difficult knowing that Alexia's body was too damaged to recover, at least she could know that these organs would make a big difference to lots of others. At that very moment there were other patients being prepped to receive a kidney or a liver or a lung or a heart or any number of the other organs. That day would mean new life for them.

The more I talked with her, the more I forgot my own fears and struggles. All of a sudden, I had a purpose for being in that room. Alexia may not be alive and need me in there, and maybe it was only a gesture to be there for Alexia's mother, but what I really recognized was that this medical team needed me right now. And they needed me to be strong and to give them my best. My job was to encourage them in the work that was before them.

The nurse and I had a good talk, and I tried to encourage her of the value that she brought to so many patients. Then we prayed together, which seemed to really bring a comforting peace. Afterward, she asked me if I would leave the OR and go upstairs with her to get Alexia. She knew that the nurses in ICU were having a difficult time over this loss and maybe I could pray with them while we were up there. I was delighted to go. We did indeed pray together upstairs before transferring Alexia to the operating room. By the time we got back downstairs, the rest of the operating room team was gathered. I was introduced to everyone and one of the doctors also thanked me for being there to support them. He then asked if I would like to watch the surgery. They pulled up a step stool so I could stand behind him, and he explained everything he was doing and about all the different parts of the body. Can you even imagine that I would be able to stand there and watch the entire surgery and miraculously it did not upset me? In fact, it was fascinating to see the human body in all its intricacies.

When the surgery was over, we prayed together, and it was such a precious time. We prayed for Alexia's spirit, and we prayed for her parents and family. We also prayed for Alexia's friends and the other girls who had been in the wreck. Finally, we prayed for each of those patients who would be blessed by receiving her organs, and we prayed for the incredible medical staff who served to make a difference in other lives.

Even as difficult as those times were, they were an incredible blessing to me. One of the biggest lessons I learned was to be aware of the fact that I am here to serve everyone around me, not just the obvious ones who need care, but also those others who are serving. And I learned that when I am focused on serving others, I forget my own fears and doubts. So, whether I am officiating a funeral or visiting someone in the hospital or handling a difficult situation, if I can intentionally focus on the other people involved and how, with God's help, I can lovingly meet their needs, then everything else will fall in place. Because when it comes down to it—it is really not about me anyway. It is about showing the love of God to others. It was through this event that my life was changed regarding my fear of hospitals and fear of things in life. God helped me to see that my fears were only when I was focused on myself, but when I keep my eyes on helping others and remember that God is with me, then it makes all the difference in the world.

Reflection Question:

When has God helped you focus on others instead of yourself?

Life in England

Divine Encounter 19

Clerical Trousers

IN THE SPRING OF 2005, I was trying to discern where God wanted me following graduation from seminary. I knew that the bishop and the cabinet were thinking about appointing me to a large church as an executive pastor. I had visited with the senior pastor of the church and it was someone that I admired and would have enjoyed working with and learning from, but I knew the position would be mainly administrative and there would not be many opportunities to preach. I certainly knew why they were considering me for that position; I had lots of management experience over large organizations from the corporate world. Yet in my heart I felt a deep sense of disappointment because I knew I had been called to preach and that was my greatest desire.

I visited with one of my professors, Dr. Bill Bryan, and explained my concern. I knew that as United Methodist clergy, we were supposed to go where we were sent. Besides, this was an incredible opportunity, at a wonderful church, with a great senior pastor, yet it just did not feel right. Bill mentioned I might be able to take part in a program with the British Methodist Church where pastors went overseas to preach and minister for a year or two. Apparently, they had a shortage of ministers and so they welcomed preachers to come over from the United States. He said I would get lots of opportunities to preach and share my love of God.

I prayed about it, investigated the option, and even visited with Bishop Moncure, who was over the North Texas Conference. I was hoping the conference would consider the position as an extension of my training so that I was better prepared to serve in a United Methodist Church when I returned. My plan was for a one-year stint and then upon returning, I would go wherever the bishop sent me.

All of the paperwork was submitted and prior to graduation I was notified I would be serving in the Rotherham / Dearne Valley Circuit under the circuit superintendent, Rev. Sean Adair. It all sounded so incredibly official and exciting. Rev. Adair sent a letter of introduction to me, along with some general information about the circuit and what it would be like to serve in England. He told me to feel free to write if I had any questions. He certainly covered all of the things a man would think was important about the job and the circuit. But he neglected to mention the critical issue of clothes. I was not sure how women in England dressed, and in particular what was acceptable for a woman preacher when she was in the pulpit.

So, I wrote back to Rev. Adair asking the important question of clothes and did women clergy wear pants in England. I received this interesting letter back, saying, "Women clergy in England do sometimes wear trousers. I am unable to address whether they wear pants. (Oh, by the way, 'pants' over here refers to underwear.)"

That was the beginning of our relationship, and Sean and I have been great friends ever since. God blessed me with lots of wonderful friends in England. What we have learned is that we do not always speak the same language, even though we all call it English, but laughter and praise is the same in any language.

I have also discovered that when I am willing to take on a challenge or do something different, like living and ministering in a foreign culture, that it becomes another chance to see God moving in new and exciting ways that I had never considered. I think sometimes we get so used to doing things a certain way that we cannot imagine that there are other ways of looking at life. Yet living in another culture or pushing yourself to do something you have never done before has a way of opening your imagination beyond anything you ever expected. You come to realize that not everyone looks at life the same way and that there are lots of new perspectives and concepts that you can learn and experience. It is not easy to step out of your comfort zone, but it is a great way to grow and develop a bigger perspective on life.

Reflection Question:

How is God redefining something you thought you understood?

Divine Encounter 20

Blessings within Disappointments

UPON ACCEPTING THE OFFER to serve as a minister overseas, I thought of my children and wondered how they would feel with me being out of the country. They both thought it sounded interesting, but particularly my son thought it was the coolest thing ever. He had spent time in England on a mission trip with the Colleyville United Methodist Church and loved the culture. He made the statement that he wished he could go with me and in the spur of the moment I said, "Well, maybe you can."

He was ecstatic about the idea. I did some checking and found that most of the others who were going over on this same program were taking their families with them, so there was no reason my son should not be able to go. I figured the education that he would gain from living abroad would make up for the year that he was delayed in finishing at the university. Besides, I liked the idea of having him with me as I ventured off to this new country.

We started working on paperwork to get everything approved for the journey. It was easy knowing what I needed to submit for myself to be approved to work in England, but I was not sure what to put down for Kevin. He would only be allowed to stay for six months if he was a tourist, so he would need to be listed as a student or a charity worker or some such designation in order to stay for the entire time.

I contacted the British Consulate for advice on how the fill out Kevin's paperwork. I thought I had done it correctly and I submitted it. In the meantime, I had left the country with the Lovers Lane UMC choir on a concert tour of China. We were gone for a few weeks and when I returned, I discovered that all of my paperwork had gone through, but Kevin's had come back with additional questions.

I was rushing to get it straightened out before we left for England in just a few days. I did not understand some of the questions that were being asked so I once again called the British Consulate number. This time I talked with someone else and when I told them what I had already

submitted they stated that I should not have submitted it under that particular designation, but instead should have used another category. So, not
knowing any better, I grabbed another form and resubmitted the information under the new designation.

As the time of our trip arrived, we were preparing for our flight to
leave for England and we had still not heard back from the British Home
Office. My paperwork was fine, and we figured if nothing else Kevin was
able to come into the country for six months as a tourist. We would try to
sort everything out after we got there.

We flew into Manchester and prepared to go through security. I was
cleared through customs, but all of a sudden, they were sending Kevin to another area. Apparently, the fact that I had submitted two documents was what
added to all of the confusion. We tried to explain that we had received two
different words of advice from the British Consulate and that it was an honest
mistake. He was not coming to the country to do anything illegal but would
be helping me in the ministry of serving the different churches.

Needless to say, it was an enduring stressful process. We were held for
five hours of questioning and when they finally released us, Kevin was told
that he would be deported back to the United States on the next plane out,
which would be the following morning. They would send him back to the
last place that he had flown from. Since we had flown from Dallas to New
York, that meant that they would fly him back to New York.

To say that we were upset is to put it mildly. Rev. Sean Adair had
been waiting for us all that time and had no idea what the delay was to get
through security. Also, all of the circuit stewards and the church people had
fixed a big breakfast for us when they had expected us five hours earlier.
They were all still waiting back at the church for us to arrive in order to give
us a grand welcome.

When we finally got there, we were exhausted, not only from the flight,
but also from the interrogation and the drive over the Pennines to get to
South Yorkshire. We shared about Kevin being ordered to fly back the next
morning and everyone was disappointed. And to be honest, I was beginning
to have doubts about whether I wanted to stay without Kevin. I had been
fine in originally planning to come over by myself, but when we decided
that he would come with me we had both gotten excited about working
together in the churches and getting to know people and traveling around to
see the sights. All of a sudden that did not seem as exciting if I were doing it
all on my own. Also, as a mother, I did not want my son to be disappointed
in not being able to stay. He had been so excited about living in England for
a year and had made all of the arrangements to be away from school. If all
of this fell through, then it would not be easy to just pick up where he left

off and continue on with his schooling. I was so very disappointed when it looked like he could not stay in England.

One of the circuit stewards was Anne Wright and she said that she and her husband, Dave, would be glad to drive us back to Manchester the following day for Kevin to catch the flight. The next morning, we began the long drive back to Manchester.

Since Kevin and I were not from England, and we did not understand all of the ramifications of what was going on, we were hesitant to question anything. But thank goodness we had Dave Wright with us. The security worker who had been so rude to us the day before was off duty, so Dave spoke with another gentleman about the matter. Dave simply explained the situation and this man was much more gracious and agreed that Kevin did not have to immediately fly back to the United States, but instead could have a few more days to try to get things sorted. Dave was definitely our hero.

Over the next few weeks, we had lots of assistance on both sides of the ocean to try to get the issue resolved. In the end, it was determined that Kevin would at least have to go back to the United States for a few days so that things could be corrected prior to his reentering England. The airline was obligated to take him back to New York and then when things were straightened out, they would bring him back from New York. It did not matter that we were originally from Texas.

As a mother I was a little concerned to be sending my son to New York without anyone to pick him up or a place to stay. I remembered that I had an aunt in New Jersey, Aunt Jenny. I gave her a call and explained the situation and she said they would be delighted to have him. They were all headed to Atlantic City for a big family reunion, and he could just fit in with everyone else.

Kevin had only been around Aunt Jenny when he was a tiny baby and perhaps at a funeral. And he had never met any of my New Jersey cousins. But he flew to New York and joined the family reunion and had a glorious time. In fact, while he was there, they took him with them to go do exciting things like parasailing and fun on the beach.

When we had originally come through New York in order to go to England, Kevin had really wanted to go to Broadway and see a show. The one he particularly wanted to see was *Wicked*. We had spent one night in New York before flying on to England, but we certainly did not have the time to go into the city in order to go to the theater. So, while he was there with all of the cousins, he asked about going to see *Wicked*. They explained to him that it was sold out for several months and there would be no way that he could get tickets. But he decided to get on the computer and try for himself. He thought that maybe a Thursday afternoon matinee might be a less busy time, and so he put that request in the computer as he searched for tickets. Sure enough, he found some tickets. They were $100 each, but he had my credit card and so he bought two of them. He then asked one of the girls, who was a newly discovered cousin about his age, if she would like to go with him. She said certainly! Everyone was shocked that he had tickets but congratulated them on the opportunity to see the highly rated musical. They caught a train into the city and made their way to the theater. He went to the will call window to collect the tickets. There seemed to be an issue with the tickets and so the woman asked the two of them to step to the side, she would sort them out in a few minutes. After the rush for sold out tickets was over, she explained to Kevin that it was July of 2005 and the tickets that he bought were for a Thursday afternoon in February of the following year. Apparently when he had put "Thursday afternoon matinee" in the computer it just went to the first one that was available—even though it was eight months away. She told him to just come back in eight months. He said he couldn't. He didn't live here and would be back in England at that time. He explained that he had used his mother's credit card to buy the tickets and had been really looking forward to seeing the musical. I guess she felt sorry for him because she told the two of them to wait for a few more minutes. She went to talk with someone and a little later a gentleman came back and asked them to follow him. He had placed two straight back chairs in the center space right behind the orchestra. He escorted the two of them out there right before the show started, and they had excellent seats to watch a musical for which most people were still waiting to get tickets.

In the end, everything was straightened out for Kevin to return to England. Looking back on it, there were lots of good things that had come out of the experience. Though it had been a big hassle, God provided an unexpected fun-filled journey to New York for Kevin. He got to know family members he had never had the opportunity to meet and he did lots of great things like parasailing and even going to see *Wicked*. Also, we certainly bonded quickly with all of those who bent over backward to help us resolve the problem, especially Dave and Anne Wright. In fact, four years later when Kevin was getting married, Dave and Anne made the trip to Texas to make sure they were there for the big event. I think it was a great reminder for us that sometimes things can become really difficult, but even in the most difficult situations there are usually some wonderful God-given blessings.

Reflection Question:

When have you seen God's blessings come from difficulties?

Divine Encounter 21

A New Prayer Ministry

MY HEART WAS VERY full having my son with me on this new experience of life in England. He was excited to learn to drive on the "wrong" side of the road. And besides, he was much better at driving a manual shift than I was, particularly with his left hand. Because I preached in a large number of different churches throughout the area, this required lots of driving. And oh, by the way, the roads in England are much, much narrower than they are in Texas. I was so glad to have Kevin with me. But Kevin only stayed for the first nine months and then he went back to Texas to be in his best friend's wedding and to get ready for starting back to college.

That meant I was back to driving on my own in England. I was pretty good at driving a car on the English roads, or at least I thought I was. I had not taken driver's education in the UK yet, but I thought I understood most of the rules.

One day I had picked up one of the other clergy, Rev. Alistair Sharp, and we were driving to our district superintendent, Rev. Vernon Marsh's home. Alistair had asked if I wanted him to drive, but I said I needed the practice so he graciously said he would ride with me. We were going down a road that was always a frustration to me. It was a particularly narrow road anyway and every so often there were these triangular "curb things" that stuck out from the side. It meant that only one car could go past that spot at a time. They always aggravated me because each time I came up to one, I had to step on the gas and go around it really quickly before another car came from the opposite direction. The first one I came to I zipped around, and Alistair sort of yelled, "What are you doing?"

I quickly explained my disgust for these stupid curbs that were sticking out in the middle of the road. About that time, I had to swerve and zip around another one of them. Alistair asked me if I knew what those "curb things" were for. I said I had no idea, but it certainly made it more difficult to go down this particular road. He laughed and said, "That is because they are supposed to slow you down and allow only one car to pass at a time."

To which I explained that since only one car could squeeze past them at a time, I was the only one who was going past it. But then he explained that the curbs were on my side of the road because I was the one who was supposed to slow down or stop and allow the other car to pass first.

"Oh!" Not much else I could say.

We arrived at Vernon's house for our meeting with the other clergy. We were to introduce ourselves and share what was new in our ministries. Alistair volunteered to go first and quickly explained that he had been strengthening his prayer life in the last little bit as he rode to the meeting with me. How nice to know that I helped move him closer to the Lord! By the way, I helped to move him even closer to God following our meeting as I got in the car and drove through the neighborhood . . . on the wrong side of the street.

Reflection Question:

What encourages you to pray more?

Divine Encounter 22

Amazing Grace

ONE OF THE MINISTRIES that we did for the community from Princess Street Methodist Church was to go to Byron Lodge Care Home once a month on a Sunday afternoon to hold a little worship service. We assembled in the gathering room, and it was a chance for us to sing a few of the old hymns and then for me to offer a short sermon.

It was usually the same group of residents already in the room when we arrived, but sometimes there were a few others who would see us come in and would join us. Also, there were a few of the regulars whose rooms we would circle by, if they were not already there, to see if they wanted to come down for the service.

Walter Cutts was the organist from Princess Street Methodist Church, and he would always come to play the keyboard. Walter had been a butcher before he retired. He is a wonderful caring man who loves the Lord and can make even that old keyboard sing. Annie Cowdell was also a member of Princess Street and has such a loving heart for the residents of the home. She would normally be there to help with the service or do it if I could not be present.

I fondly remember one Sunday afternoon when we arrived at Byron Lodge for the service. Walter started messing with the keyboard; it sometimes had a mind of its own. Today was apparently one of those days. Something was not working correctly on it. One of the sweet little ladies had requested that we sing "Amazing Grace." When Walter started playing there was somehow a rumba beat underneath the notes he was playing. Have you ever heard "Amazing Grace" with a rumba beat? It was hilarious, but Walter kept on playing and the people kept on singing.

One of the fascinating things about musicology is the fact that someone may have learned a hymn when he or she was a child and even if they have had a stroke or Alzheimer's or lose the ability to speak, they can still sing all of the words to the song. This is especially true in the case of old hymns that also have a special spiritual connection for someone. If someone has had a close relationship with the Lord in the past and those experiences were enhanced with liturgy or certain hymns, then later those words or music can ignite an emotion that bubbles to the surface and once again awakens the memories and feelings. It has a way of touching something deep inside of us. Also, for many people, music is just a powerful way to praise and worship God and draw us nearer to the Lord.

That was definitely the case for this wonderful group of people gathered together on this day. Most of them had been lost in their own worlds without any awareness of what was going on around them. But as soon as Walter began playing "Amazing Grace" it was as if the entire room awoke and they began singing with all of their hearts—even if it was to the strange beat from the old keyboard.

Over on the far side of the room was a dear woman; I think her name was Gladys. Each time I came, I would lean down and speak to her, but she would never give any acknowledgment that she heard me. However, as soon as we started singing one of the old hymns she knew and loved, she would start yelling at the top of her lungs, "Oh, yeah! Oh, yeah! Oh, yeah!"

I want to make sure you have the full picture of everything that was going on in that room that day, because I know the Holy Spirit was enjoying the excitement of the moment. It was Walter play "Amazing Grace" with a rumba beat (and amazingly keeping a straight face as if it was the most natural thing in the world to put the two rhythms together), about ten to twelve wonderful elderly people all singing their own words to the hymn as loudly as they possibly could (they got most of the words right), Gladys was yelling "Oh, yeah!" over and over, and to be honest—I was laughing so hard that I could not get the words out. I expected any moment for some of the residents to pull out their lighters and wave them back and forth in the air and possibly for someone to toss a beach ball or throw a Frisbee across the room. In that instant it was the most surreal experience I have ever had, and the realization of the fact that here I am in South Yorkshire singing "Amazing Grace" with one of the sweetest congregations ever was truly endearing. I could imagine God smiling as we sang his praise.

Reflection Question:

Where have you seen the joy of worshiping God?

Chapter 23

When God Shakes Our World

THERE ARE TIMES WHEN those in ministry start feeling like they are running dry. Maybe it is after they have pushed themselves for too long, without taking any time for renewal. Or maybe it is because they are not staying close to the Lord through Bible study and prayer. Or perhaps, it is just all the other things that are going on in life that finally gets to them. But sometimes you just start doubting your relationship with the Lord and if you can continue leading other people. Maybe it is because you pour so much of yourself into pastoral care for those who are sick and dying and going through crisis situations, that you start feeling drained.

While I was in England, there were a couple of times where I was struggling with questions of whether my ministry really made any difference. I felt lonely and depressed. I remember one time in particular where it had rained for almost an entire week. I would usually go out and run every day, but it wasn't my favorite thing to do in the rain. Running every day and eating right are two things that help me stay on an even keel. And of course, some of the biggest things that help are praying, studying Scripture, and counting my blessings. Yet this week I was apparently off on all of my spiritual and physical disciplines and it was definitely impacting my attitude.

Even though I was aware of what was going on for me, I was having a hard time inspiring myself. I kept thinking that I just needed to feel God's presence and then it would be OK. "Lord, why can't I feel you? Why can't I experience you?"

The next day would be Wednesday and every Wednesday in my village of Wath-upon-Dearne was market day. Market day in an English village is where everything comes alive because the vendors show up on the market square and set up their variety of booths and stores. Everyone who lives in the area comes in for the day to do their shopping and handle their business. Since it was market day, Trinity Methodist Church would always have Holy Communion at 8:30 a.m. followed by Coffee Morning at 9:00 a.m. There was a large sign in front of the church advertising both events. The Holy Communion portion was primarily attended by our members, but our deepest hope was that others in the community would decide to join us for the short service. I would usually give a short devotional and then we would partake of Holy Communion. Following that, we would walk over to the hall next door and prepare for Coffee Morning. Coffee Morning was a time when we would open up our hall for several hours and serve tea or coffee and baked goods for the shoppers who wanted to take a little break and sit inside at the tables and visit. Lots of people stopped by for Coffee Morning, but unfortunately, they rarely attended the service beforehand.

I was already thinking about the Communion service the next morning. The last couple of weeks our attendance had not been good. It was disappointing when I felt that I could not inspire new people into a relationship with the Lord. I was beginning to wonder if I was keeping the longtime Christians motivated in their faith. Actually, I was starting to doubt everything in my life and faith. My head was filled with ruminations, such as, why did I come all the way to this country where it rains all the time? I missed the sunshine and big sky of Texas. I was missing my children. I wanted to talk with my beautiful daughter, LeeRand, and to know everything that was going on in her life. I wanted to check up on Kevin and see how his classes were going. I was afraid my children would forget me or think that their mother abandoned them. Let's admit it, I was homesick, but most of all, I was missing God.

It seemed as if I was just going through the motions, yet God was not there. I no longer knew what to say to other people to inspire them and help them draw nearer to the Lord. While I was worried about inspiring others, I realized I was feeling disconnected from God myself.

In a state of despair, I found myself lying in bed, crying, and trying so hard to pray to God and be heard. Finally, I cried out to God and said, "Lord, if you are still in my life, then I need to know it. I need to feel that you are here with me. Shake up my world and let me know that you are still God and that I am still yours." And believe it or not . . . it felt like the room was shaking. It was as if something was moving my bed, but at the same time I was sort of aware of other little things in the room sort of tinkering back and forth. It went on for just a few seconds, but it was astounding.

Afterward I lay very still thinking, "Oh Lord, wow, that was so cool! Did I just imagine that, or did you do it for me? You gave me an earthquake to shake up my world! How amazing is that!"

Whatever doldrums or depression I might have had before, believe me it was gone now! I had just felt the earth move under my feet (or really under my entire bed and body). That was God! He was listening to and answering my prayer. I could not wait to share what God did in my bedroom as he shook me into action. I now knew what my devotional would be about tomorrow—God hears and answers prayers and shakes up our world!

The next morning, I got over to the church early as I looked forward to people coming in so that I could share my testimony. The first one walked in the door and as soon as she stepped in the sanctuary the first thing she said was, "My goodness, did you feel the earthquake last night?" Someone else was coming in right behind her and also said something about the earthquake. I was shocked! I thought that was my own personal earthquake to shake me out of my complacency and get me motivated and back into ministry. Yet everyone that walked in that morning, and we did have a good crowd, could not wait to talk about the earthquake. One thing I learned was even though earthquakes are common in California, they are not in England!

Was it just a coincidence that there was an earthquake at the very same moment that I was praying that God would shake up my world? Did God respond to my prayer by giving the earthquake or was it the other way around? Did God direct me to think those thoughts and pray that prayer, knowing that he was about to send an earthquake? I'm not sure, but what I do know is that I was struggling in my ministry and I needed to feel God . . . and I certainly did. Maybe I really did not want to claim too much that I was the one who was praying for things to be shaken up, after all, there may be someone who ended up with structural damage and I don't want them suing me for my prayers!

Reflection Question:

When has God shaken things up in your life?

Divine Encounter 24

The Gate Is Narrow

WATH-UPON-DEARNE WAS THE VILLAGE I lived in while in England. Outside of it was a small lake. Most mornings I would get up early and go running around the lake a few times. It was always great to be out at the lake in the early hours with few people around.

The weather and the lighting conditions were always changing. In the summer the sun would come up at 4:00 a.m. and in the winter it would be closer to 9:00 a.m. Also, the weather could be foggy or pouring rain or snow. And then there's the time of the year when the midges are out. I was not familiar with midges before moving to England. They say everything is bigger in Texas and so even our gnats were bigger than midges.

If you have never been around midges they are teeny tiny little flying bugs that all swarm together so that they form sort of a little dark cloud. If you run through them, they get in your eyes and nose and mouth and hair—you get the idea. Of course, my favorite time to run around the lake was when the weather was just right and the sun was coming up, and definitely when there were no midges!

One morning I had gone out to run and the midges were particularly bad. I definitely had to keep my mouth closed as I was running, and it was tough to see. I would close one eye and then peak out of the other. Most of the path around the lake I had run so many times that I knew exactly how it went. A small portion of it was paved sidewalk, but most of it was just dirt trail. One area where the pavement begins has two poles set about three feet apart and a sign saying the path is restricted to foot traffic (no horses or motor vehicles).

As I was coming up to that particular part of the path, I knew the wide pavement coming up would be smooth. The midges were particularly bad in that area so I glanced ahead to judge where the opening was between the two poles. I then closed my eyes to avoid the "midge assault." Unfortunately, I misjudged the space between the poles because instead of going between them I ran smack into solid metal. I bounced backward like a rag doll and lay sprawled on the ground. It took a moment for me to realize what had just happened. Not even checking to see if I had injured myself, I immediately jumped up and looked around hoping that no one saw me. How embarrassing! All I could do was laugh at myself.

As I stood there looking at the two poles and the narrow space between them, I smiled and a Scripture passage came to mind: "Small is the gate and narrow is the road that leads to life, and few find it" (Matt 7:14). It was a good reminder that you need to keep your eyes open, so you know where you are going. God will guide us in life, yet it is important to remain focused so that we stay on the right path.

Reflection Question:

Where is God leading you and are you focused?

Divine Encounter 25

Thinking They Know

SOMETIMES WE MAKE THE assumption that everyone knows who Jesus Christ is and that if they have not decided to follow him it is just because that is their choice. But what if people really do not know who he is and what a difference he can make in their lives? What if even in those societies and in those places where we think the knowledge of the Lord is commonplace . . . that it really is not?

A member of one of the circuit churches invited me to come to the school where she works to talk to the RE class (Religious Education). The young people in this particular class were all about thirteen to fourteen years old and she thought it would be good for them to hear about Christianity from a clergy. She also thought that they might have some questions about life in America.

We make assumptions about things based on what we know. Thus, I walked into the class imagining all the things they were probably studying about the Christian faith. I assumed they would have a vast knowledge of Christianity whether or not they accepted it. After all, this was a Religious Education class. After I was introduced to the class of about thirty students, my plan was to start with whatever they were learning. So, I began by asking what they had already studied about Christianity. One of them answered that they knew all about it. He then proceeded to tell me that there is a nave and an altar and a pulpit and baptismal font and buttresses. I quickly realized that they had been studying Christian cathedrals and thus they could name the architectural elements. I told the student it is wonderful that they knew all of the architectural information. But then I asked what they could tell me about the Christian faith. The entire class just sat there with a blank look. I said, "Tell me what you know about God." Silence.

"Ok, what about Jesus?" Nothing. I finally asked, "Do you know who Christ Jesus is?" A young man in the back of the room raised his hand and said with all sincerity, "Christ—does that have anything to do with

Christmas?" My heart broke as I realized they did not know the story of Jesus—who he is and how he came to save their lives. At that point, I started with Christmas and explained about his birth and went on from there. But I could tell from the students' faces, as well as the young teacher's face, that this was all new information to them.

I don't know if this is typical for RE classes, or if I just happened to stumble into the one where the teacher did not know anything about Christianity other than the architecture of the cathedrals. But I found it also disturbing that young people of this age did not even know the true meaning of Christmas. And I'm sure that is not just an issue for England but is true in the United States and lots of other places around the world.

Sometimes we don't bother sharing the good news because we are speculating that if people really wanted to hear about it, they would walk into a church or pick up a Bible or ask someone. We forget that maybe they don't even know enough about Jesus Christ to begin asking questions.

We are clearly instructed by Jesus to go make disciples of all nations,[1] which means we cannot just sit back and assume that people know about the Lord. And we also have a special responsibility to the next generation to make sure that they are taught the true good news. How alarming it is to know that someone could be placed in a position to teach a group of young people a topic as important as Religious Education and yet they themselves do not even understand the basics of Christianity. And what a shame it is for us in the church that we are not following up to make sure that the good news is actually shared.

Yes, my young friend, Christ does have something to do with Christmas. In fact, there is no Christmas—or hope for life—without Jesus Christ.

Reflection Question:

When have you assumed someone already knew the glory of God?

1. Matt 28:19.

Divine Encounter 26

A Different Perspective

THROUGHOUT MY LIFE (AND particularly throughout the last fifteen years), I have been blessed to travel. I feel so honored to be able to meet people from various cultures and get a glimpse of life (and God) through their eyes. We are all alike in that we are God's children and we have the basic wants and desires for health and provisions—food, clean water, shelter, and certainly love!

Yet for all the ways we are the same, there are also cultural distinctions that impact how we look at life. They are neither good nor bad, that's just how it is, based on what we have learned from our point of view. Particularly in those countries where I have had the opportunity to spend more time, it has been a chance to gain additional insight. I have had the privilege to travel to twenty-four countries, and in about a third of them I have spent extensive time, usually staying with friends, encountering the culture more deeply. Even though I am not a sociologist, it is certainly interesting to observe what people pay attention to and how they support and love each other. Since I lived in the UK for four years, there were lots of fun comparisons and "aha" moments.

After I had been living in England for about two years, someone asked me how long I could drive using my American driver's license before I needed to get a British driver's license. Wow! Good question. I had never really thought about it. I felt like I was a pretty good driver (well, except those times when I increased Alistair's prayer life with my driving skills). I started checking and realized that I should have already taken lessons and passed my exam for a British driver's license. Oops!

I decided I better get busy. No big deal. I would just take lessons, and it would be easy since I already knew how to drive, and I would go pass the test. But then I started hearing horror stories of how many tries it had taken different people to pass their driving exams—sixteen times, twenty-one times, some were still working on it. Oh, my goodness! Maybe this was not as easy as I thought it would be.

I found a gentleman who would give me driving lessons. It was a pay-by-the-hour arrangement, and it was not cheap (or as my English friends would say, "It was dear."). I started my lessons a couple of days a week in his car, which had a manual transmission.

OK, a point of clarification, my first car way back in the 1970s had a manual transmission. But the steering wheel was on the correct side of the car, and so I was shifting with my right hand. After that first car, every other car from then on was wonderfully blessed with an automatic transmission. I can drive a manual transmission, but it certainly is not my preference! In fact, when I had first come to England and Kevin and I were learning our way around and how to drive on the opposite side of the road, the car that the circuit gave us had a manual transmission. It took a little getting used to, but I could certainly drive it to wherever I needed to go. But about a year and a half into my time in the UK, the engine just stopped. Unfortunately, it did it while I was in the center lane of the M1 (a major highway) during a busy time of the day—not a good thing. Some blokes in a van pulled up behind me and helped me safely push my car to the edge of the motorway. That was the end of that car.

So, when I was going to purchase a car to continue driving in England, I decided that the next one would definitely have an automatic transmission. I also wanted a larger car so that I would feel safer, and when my friends and family came to visit, we could easily fit all of their luggage in the car. A good friend from one of the circuit churches, Keith Rutherford, said that he would help me find a car. He was a knowledgeable and patient friend who was willing to take me to the different car places to find just the right car for me. I especially liked the car he was driving, so I figured he would be a great asset in my search. In the end, we found a beautiful baby blue Rover with an automatic transmission. Ah, life is good!

I really wanted to take the driving lessons in my own car since it was so much easier to drive, but the driving instructor pointed out that if I took the driving test in a car with an automatic transmission, then my license would be restricted to cars with automatic transmissions only. Yet if I took it in a car with a manual transmission, I would be able to drive all cars.

"Well, OK." I convinced myself I could do this.

But there was another little issue. Since I was beyond the time when I should have gotten a British driver's license, officially I should have a sign with a big L on it in the rear window of the car. Argh! L stood for Learner, but it felt more like Loser! Also, if you have an L sign in the car, you have to have an experienced licensed driver riding with you at all times. Now this was beginning to cramp my style. It meant that when I had preaching and speaking engagements all over the place, I had to find someone with a license to ride to all of the events with me. I desperately needed to hurry up and get my driver's license.

While I was taking these driving lessons, it was getting more and more frustrating. Even though I had driven a manual shift before, apparently, I did not do the footwork exactly like the British are taught to do it. It worked my way, but it was not "proper," and my instructor explained that I would not pass. I kept trying, but the pressure in the meantime of always having to have someone with me for all the various engagements was getting harder and harder. I finally told him I just needed to take the driving test in my own car and that I was fine with just having a driver's license that was limited to cars with an automatic transmission.

I had already taken all of the tests that you have to take online about the signs and rules and safety and simulation. I had passed all of those. But now it was time for the infamous driving portion.

In order to take the test, you have to go online and book a location, date, and time. Like a lot of other things in England (including crematoriums) I was shocked by how long the wait is before you can get a slot. I found one that was a little distance away, but at least it was the closest date. It was three weeks away. That meant for three more weeks I would have to rally all my different friends and church members to ride with me to different places where I would be speaking. My test date certainly could not come soon enough! Besides that, there is a charge of 50£ (the equivalent of a $100) each time you book a test. I was ready to get all of this over and just get back to doing ministry!

The day before the driving test I was excited, but also nervous about taking it. Knowing the power of prayer, I decided to email some of my friends and explain the situation and ask them to be in prayer for me. I intentionally chose five friends from Texas and five from the UK. I said that I would be taking the driving test the following morning, and I would really appreciate their prayers. I heard from all of them saying they definitely would be praying for me.

When the big day arrived, the driving instructor came to my house, and we rode together in my car to the site where the exams are taken. There were lots of other drivers there with their own driving instructors waiting to take their tests as well. My examiner called out my name, and I held up my hand. She looked me over as if she was not sure I was worthy to be taking this exam, and with clipboard in hand asked where the car was. Most of the other cars were the various driving instructor's cars, but there was my big baby blue Rover. I explained I wanted to take the test in my car, and I did know that it would restrict me to a driver's license which was limited to cars with automatic transmissions.

My driving instructor, along with all of the other instructors, stood at the doorway of the building and watched as all of their students walked away with the different examiners. The examiner walked with me to my car. For some reason, I had the feeling she was not too excited to be the one who had to test the American and especially in this big car. She told me to get in and sit behind the wheel. I followed her instructions. And then she started walking around the car over and over, kicking tires and looking at everything. I began thinking maybe it would have been a good idea if I had taken the exam in my driving instructor's car. She did not look happy.

Finally, she came to the driver's door and told me to get out. She informed me that my back, left tire did not have enough tread on it, and I had five minutes to change the tire. What?! It looked perfectly fine to me, but she didn't like the looks of it. I had changed one car tire in my life and that was when my father was teaching me how to do it when I was a teenager. Ever since then God has blessed me to have someone else who had more expertise to be around. I thought to myself that there was no way I could change the tire in just five minutes. She saw the shock on my face and repeated that I had five minutes to change the tire or I would lose my testing slot, and I would have to try to get another one. I certainly knew what that meant—going back online and finding another testing slot a month or two away and paying another 50£.

All of the driving instructors who were standing in the doorway heard what she was telling me and about five or six of them rushed over in mass and said they would change my tire, and it would be done super quick. They graciously started swarming around the car to handle it. I had never even looked at the spare, but I had thought before they even opened the trunk that since everything else in this country is smaller than it is in Texas, that with my luck it would be one of those tiny temporary tires. Sure enough, when they pulled up the panel in the boot (trunk) that was what it was.

I said to wait just a moment before they went to all that trouble. I asked her as she stood there watching everything with her arms crossed, "Since it is a smaller temporary tire, if they change it, am I still able to take the test and will I have the possibility of passing?"

All eyes were on the examiner. And she said, "No! You cannot take the motorway portion of the test with the temporary tire."

I took a deep breath and then turned around and sincerely thanked all of the gentlemen who had tried to come to my rescue. "I truly appreciate all of your assistance, but apparently today is not my day." I tried to be as gracious as I could to the examiner and thanked her for her time. I figured it would not be in anyone's interest if I threw a temper tantrum or started crying. It would just reflect badly on me as an American woman. I did not particularly agree with the way I was treated, but I was not the one in authority and I just needed to humbly accept it and move on.

My instructor and I got back in my car to leave the testing facility. I was trying really hard not to cry or to let my emotions show. (To be honest, if I had been by myself, I would have driven away to some remote place and I would have had a major screaming, pounding on the steering wheel, kicking the tire tantrum. But the instructor was with me, so I was making it my challenge to be calm and cool.)

Since I was obligated to pay the instructor for a two-hour session anyway, I asked if he would mind if we went to a tire store. I knew in order to go to one, since I had the L on the back of my car, I would have to have someone ride with me, so it might as well be him. He said he would be glad to do so. We drove to a tire dealership in Rotherham and I pulled up in front. A gentleman came out and asked how he could be of assistance. I simply pointed at the car and said that I would like four brand new tires.

My instructor quickly spoke up and said, "No, you don't need four, you just need one on the back left."

I looked at him and said, "Believe me, I want FOUR new tires. That will never happen to me again."

So that is how I got new tires for my car. But that is not the end of the story. When I finally got home from the disappointing, expensive day, I still had to go online and see if I could get another testing slot. I knew last time I had been really fortunate to get a slot that was just three weeks away and I had not had to drive an extremely long way to get to the testing location. I cringed thinking about how much longer I would have to try to convince people to ride places with me, so I prayed as I opened the website to get a slot for a test. To my complete surprise and delight, there was a location not too far away which happened to have a cancelation in a few days. After that, it did not have another opening for a couple of months. I grabbed the slot and happily paid my 50£. I was just delighted to not have to wait a really long time.

Afterward I remembered that I had asked my ten friends to be praying for me. I really was hoping I could just send them an email that said, "Passed! Celebrate!" But today was not the day for that. Instead it was a much longer email explaining the tire situation, but in the end, I shared that I had four new tires and that I had just gotten another testing slot for a few days from then and that I would truly, truly appreciate lots of prayers for this next adventure.

I am extremely thankful for friends who love me and are willing to pray for me. The fascinating thing is that I heard from all ten of them and there was a pattern to their replies. The five from England all sent very gracious notes saying how very sorry they were that I did not pass and that it had been so difficult. Some of them even told their own horror stories or about the difficulties they or someone else had. But all five of the return emails from Texas said something simple like, "Congratulations! You have four new tires! I'm sure you will do great next time. Love you!"

Maybe it was just a fluke, but it was interesting that one group of friends would focus on compassion and empathy and commiseration, while the other group figured there was some piece of celebration in the news. I saw God in all of the responses. But it made me wonder if we are culturally conditioned to look at life a certain way, and are we even aware that there might be other ways to view a situation? It has been a good lesson for me to consider other options of how I respond to situations. And particularly, where is God in that event and what can I learn that will glorify him?

And, oh by the way, I did pass the next driving test! Woohoo!

Reflection Question:

How do you respond to disappointment?

Divine Encounter 27

Daring to Touch

THE GREATEST THING WE can do is to touch another life with the love of Jesus. But also, sometimes that is one of the hardest things to do—to dare to reach out to someone.

When I lived in Wath-upon-Dearne, I would get up very early, almost every morning, and would run to a lake outside the village, run around the lake a couple of times and then run back home. There was a group of homeless men who were often somewhere in the village center at night or early in the morning. Often, they would be gathered behind one of the shops that I would pass. They would usually be having a few drinks and I never knew if it was a continuation from the drinking party the night before, or if they were just up early and beginning their day with a little taste of alcohol. I would always wave at them when I ran past and would sometimes stop to visit.

For over a year and a half, anytime I visited with them, I would invite them to church. Of course, their response was that the church people would never want them to come. I always assured them that this church would welcome them anytime they decided to attend. I knew that was true because I had heard the church people talk about how much they wished others would come visit the church. So, I knew they would be welcomed with open arms.

Phil was the leader of the group and the two of us had visited several times. From the questions he asked I began to believe that he really wanted to know God. I knew that if Phil ever decided to accept Jesus as his Savior and come to church it would be an encouragement for the others as well.

One morning I was up very early running when I saw the guys out there enjoying the sunrise and their beverage of choice. I stopped to say hello to them. I mentioned again that they were always welcome at our church. I reminded them that it was Wednesday, and we had Holy Communion and a devotional at 8:30 a.m. and then the regular Coffee Morning at 9:00 a.m. They were certainly welcome to both. I got the usual response of friendly banter about the fact that they were not church people and that they would never be welcomed. I tried to assure them that the invitation was genuine. I ran on home to get ready for the Communion service.

To my surprise about an hour later when I came out of the manse to go to the Communion service, Phil and two of his friends were sitting at the front door of the church waiting to go in. I was delighted! They said they wanted to give it a try if I was sure that it was OK. I reiterated once again they were welcome. I opened the door and told them to make themselves at home and that I had to go behind the chancel area to get the Communion elements ready.

When I came out of the sacristy, I saw them sitting on the back pew of this huge sanctuary. I yelled back to them and told them to come to the front row. I explained that we normally only had a little over a dozen people on Wednesday mornings and that they all sat on the front row and we were very informal. Phil and his buddies moved to the front row and sat down all ready for things to start happening. About that time the door opened, and the church members started to come in. I watched their faces as they entered and were so surprised that someone other than the usual group was there. But when they walked up to the front row and saw who it was, their expressions changed. They all knew Phil and the other guys.

If you grow up in a small village, you usually stay there. They had all gone to school with each other and had known each other all their lives. They had just taken different paths. My church members normally sat across the entire front row. This morning, however, they stayed exclusively on the right side. Phil and his buddies occupied the left. Not one single church member came over to greet them and say how delighted they were they were there. Instead they filled up the first row on the right side, and then started filling up the second row.

As I watched what was happening, my heart began to break. Here I had promised these guys that they would be welcomed and loved, and yet I did not see a whole lot of love being extended to them. I kept chitchatting with everyone as they came in and with Phil and the guys hoping that everyone would get the feeling that we were all in this together.

It was time to start the service. Whatever devotional I had planned to give went quickly out the window and instead I talked about how in heaven we will all gather around one table and share in the feast. I noted that God put us in this world together to love each other and support each other and that we were all God's children.

Finally, it came time for Holy Communion, and the way the church normally received Communion was just to come and kneel and be served the bread and juice and go back to their seats and the next group would come forward. But all of a sudden, I felt like God was saying to do things a little differently this time. Since it was a small group on Wednesdays, they could all spread out along the altar rail and be served at the same time. But instead, I instructed them all to come forward at once and said half of them should go ahead and kneel in preparation to receive the body and blood of Christ and the other half should stand behind one of the individuals who was kneeling. I asked the ones who were standing behind each person to just very lightly place their hands on the shoulders of the person in front of them and be in prayer for that person as they received Holy Communion. Then after I had served all of those who were kneeling, I would say a blessing for them. They would then swap; and the ones who had been standing behind could now kneel while the others stood behind them and very lightly touched their shoulders and prayed for them as they received.

I had never done Holy Communion like that, but I knew God was telling me how it should be done. And so, I told them to come forward. I watched as Phil and his buddies rushed to the altar rail and knelt. I don't know if they had ever received Holy Communion before, but they were hungry for it and hungry to experience whatever God had for them that morning. They knelt and bowed their heads and closed their eyes. And then I watched my church members whom I loved so dearly, it was as if they did not know what to do. They sort of stumbled over each other trying to decide who would kneel and who would stand behind whom. And it meant that three of them needed to come to this side and stand behind Phil and the others. I watched as this attractive, elderly, prim and proper English woman, Kathlene, came over and stood behind Phil. Here she was with her beautiful, perfectly coiffed, silver white hair and her pink sweater and white blouse, and here was Phil kneeling at the altar rail with his long, stringy, greasy hair hanging all the way down to his shoulder and his dirty clothes. I watched as she struggled to place her hands on his shoulders, but when she did, I saw something about her transform, and it was as if something wonderful was flowing into her. I watched as tears started streaming down her face while at the same time, she had the most beautiful smile as though she was experiencing something amazing. I truly saw God in that moment.

I started serving the Communion bread on the far end and came to where Phil was, and when I called his name and said, "This is Christ's body broken for you," he looked up at me with these sparkling eyes that seemed to be soaking up the full glory of the moment, and it was obvious that he had been crying as well. I finished serving the Communion wine (juice) to the first row and then said a blessing over them. I told them to swap places with those who had been praying for them and now it was their time to pray for the others. I watched as all of them swapped with their partners, but particularly I watched as Kathlene and Phil switched places. He had been so excited to receive Communion, but now he could not wait to pray for Kathlene. She knelt and I watched, with my heart stopping just a little bit, as I saw him place his filthy hands on that lovely light pink sweater. I said to touch very lightly, but it was obvious that Phil was paying a lot more attention to the prayer part than the part about touching lightly. His eyes were closed, and he was just pouring out silent prayers for her. And as I served, I could almost see the power of Jesus flow from Kathlene to Phil as she ate the bread and drank the wine. I said a final blessing for this group and watched as Kathlene stood up, and she and Phil took one look at each other and just wrapped their arms around each other and stood there laughing and crying and both were overwhelmed with something that they had both experienced. They both shared that there was some kind of electric power that moved through them as they prayed for each other.

That experience changed Kathlene and Phil that day, but it also changed our church and our community. From then on that was how people wanted to partake of Holy Communion—in a way that recognized that none of us come to the table alone, yet we have the privilege to be there with all people because we all need Jesus. Phil ended up accepting Jesus and was baptized on Christmas Day and joined the church. He had an opportunity to be a witness to others who would have never listened to a pastor or someone from the church, but because they saw how his life was changed, others wanted what he had.

God put us all in this life together for a reason. And one of the most glorious things we can do is to be the connection that brings others closer to Christ. Don't miss out on reaching out to others in love and letting them know that Jesus Christ is there to touch them and meet their needs. I can assure you, when you are willing to be used by God to touch someone else's life, you will feel the power of the Holy Spirit moving in your own.

Reflection Question:

When have you been willing to reach out and touch someone?

Divine Encounter 28

An Opportunity to Preach

In the United Methodist Church, clergy are appointed by the bishop and the cabinet to serve in a particular church. As I was graduating from seminary, I had heard that I would probably be appointed as an executive pastor at a large church because of my previous experience managing organizations in the business world. It was a fabulous opportunity, but I truly felt that I had been called to the ministry to preach. And so, I requested permission to go to the UK where there was a shortage of preachers.

When I originally went to England, the plan was to only stay for one year. I told Bishop Moncure that I just wanted the opportunity to preach, and then I would come back and was willing to go wherever I was appointed. But as I got involved with the ministry in England, I realized that they had a real need for more preachers. If you are not familiar with the Methodist system in the UK, areas are divided into circuits. Ministers are not appointed to an individual church, but instead to a circuit made up of several churches.

I was appointed to the Rotherham / Dearne Valley Circuit, which is located in South Yorkshire. Several circuits make up a district, and we were a part of the Sheffield District. Within the circuit that I originally went, there were twenty-two churches and seven ordained clergy. Obviously, there is no way that only seven clergy can cover all twenty-two churches every Sunday, so in addition to the ordained clergy, there are usually local preachers who are lay people who have been trained to preach. They cannot officiate over Holy Communion, but the local preachers can lead services and they do a great job preaching. Each quarter a preaching plan is published for the circuit showing all of the churches for all of the Sundays for three months and the preacher (either ordained or local) assigned to each of the services. Sometimes, even with the local preachers, there are not enough preachers to cover all of the churches. In those cases, two churches will have to join together, or a church will have to make their own arrangements.

I realized very quickly that there was a shortage of preachers, not only in the Methodist Church, but also in virtually all of the Christian denominations in England. As my first year came to a close, I really struggled as to whether I should go back to Texas and the United Methodist Church where I knew there was an overabundance of pastors. (In fact, they were not all being commissioned or appointed because there were so many.) By comparison, in England many churches had difficulties finding a pastor to cover all of their services and needs. I did not want to go against my promise to return, but at the same time I could really see the desperate need for more clergy and felt that God was calling me to stay in England a little longer.

I had come over in hopes of preaching, and I was certainly having that opportunity. According to the preaching plan, I was scheduled every Sunday morning and evening to a different church within our circuit. But in addition to preaching in the Methodist churches per the plan, I was also constantly being asked by other denominations if I would come preach at their churches on a Sunday afternoon or late evening.

The other churches would usually call several weeks before to make sure they were on my calendar (or diary as the English would say). If it was a special service such as a Harvest Service or an Anniversary Service, then they might request a specific Scripture or topic for the sermon. At first, I was only preaching one other service each Sunday besides my scheduled Methodist churches. But soon the load increased, and it was not unusual for me to preach at four to five different churches on a Sunday. I would preach, as well as lead, a different service for each of them. I was certainly getting my practice both writing and preaching, but I loved every minute of it. I truly felt that I was doing what I was called to do. I had known from the very beginning that I had to share with others about this amazing God who loves us and is with us every moment of the day. I was capable of handling the administrative business of the church, as well as the pastoral and counseling portion; but to be honest, my heart was in studying Scripture, listening to God, and then preaching and sharing what God had given me.

I realized the most important thing I could do was spend my time preparing sermons and preaching, rather than being distracted by all the paperwork and administrative duties. I ended up hiring a member of one of my congregations, Pat Hutchinson. I set up an office for her in my home and split my salary with her. She handled the administration portion of the ministry, which freed me up to focus more on preaching. It was an incredible blessing to have Pat's help, and she became one of my dearest friends. Her love and support helped me to be very intentional in sharing the good news and to focus on where I felt I could make the biggest difference.

Besides having more opportunities to preach each week, the word soon got out to a lot of community groups that I would be glad to come and give a talk for their meetings. I often received phone calls asking if I was that "tall, blonde woman who talked with the funny accent." Sometimes they would know I was American, but I was surprised how many people also guessed Canadian. (I'm not sure how you confuse a Texas accent for a Canadian one.) They would then ask if I would come speak to their organization. When I asked what they would like for me to talk about, they either said that it did not matter—they just wanted to hear my accent, or they would ask me to explain why I was in England. Either way, it was a great opportunity to share my testimony of what God had done in my life and how the Lord had led me to where I was at that time. It was fascinating that they would extend an invitation for me to come speak to their organizations when they normally would not consider inviting an English pastor or vicar. I always considered it was God's way of opening a door for me to witness to my faith.

In the end, I served for four years in England, and it was an amazing experience. I had wanted to preach, and God certainly provided lots of op-portunities. I also had the chance to make some incredible friends scattered throughout a variety of churches and communities. But there finally came a time when I knew I needed to return to Texas. It was a hard decision to make since I could still see the need for ministry in England, and yet I also knew that I had family responsibilities and ministry commitments back home.

I truly missed seeing my precious children. I also knew my dear father was getting older and I was worried about him. And I missed my brother and other family members and good friends. Yet when I left England, I felt like a part of my heart was left there. Looking back on the time that I was there, I am touched by how God opened up so many opportunities for me to travel and preach and meet so many extraordinary people.

I am definitely someone who gets very attached to other people in a short period of time. God has blessed me with friends from all over the world, but especially in those areas where I have lived and served and shared God-experiences. Sometimes it feels like I leave a part of me in each place, which makes it difficult as I move on to the next location because I am still praying for and connected with those in my past. I heard a good illustration for this the other day. Someone was talking about those Matryoshka dolls (Russian nesting dolls) where they all look alike and normally there are several inside of each other. It is as if the dolls which represent me have been taken apart and each time that I leave a location, I leave one of them—or a part of me there with those people. I realized that it is frustrating for me because I can never put myself fully back together because I feel my heart is spread out over so many places. Yet then I thought about it, and I realized that with all of these individuals and communities that I love so dearly, most of them know the Lord. In fact, God is the most intimate and magnificent part of what we have shared together. If nothing else, someday we will all be in heaven together, and I have a feeling that is when I will feel complete and whole and put back together just the way God wants. And until then . . . I guess I'll just keep preaching and reaching out to more of God's precious people.

Reflection Question:

What has God called you to be very intentional about doing?

Back in Texas

A Precious Gift

I REMEMBER BEING IN England at the time when I heard from my older brother, Mark Harrison, that he and his wife, Linda, were going to be grandparents. They were so excited! Their only son, Gray, and his wife, Maddie, would be expecting their first child in September. Mark and Linda were beginning to contemplate what grandparent names they wanted to be called by this precious child. (They later settled on Pops and Omah.) At the same time, Maddie and Gray were starting to get things ready for this new addition to the family.

In the preparations for the baby there were family and friends who hosted baby showers so that they could help with the endless supply of things that a baby will need: diapers and wipes, bottles and outfits, blankets and toys, and the list goes on. But one of the unusual gifts was from a neighbor who happened to be a doctor. That gift was the opportunity to have a more detailed sonogram so they could know more about their baby. They had already had one sonogram and it let them know that it was a little boy. But it would be interesting to see if this other more detailed sonogram had any other exciting news about their unborn son.

When Maddie and Gray went for the more in-depth sonogram it certainly showed more detail, but it was not what they expected. What they learned was that the baby had a congenital heart defect. This had not been discovered prior to this sonogram but thank goodness it was discovered beforehand so precautions could be put in place to handle the situation as soon as he was born. This tiny baby would need open-heart surgery soon after his birth, but there was every expectation that the surgeons could resolve the issue.

Keegan Holt Harrison was born on September 12, 2007. Maddie actually gave birth to Keegan in a Plano hospital, and he was quickly life-flighted to Children's Medical Center in Dallas. The following day Keegan had open-heart surgery. It was a ten-hour operation on a tiny heart no larger than a walnut. The doctors thought they had corrected the issue, but when problems persisted, they needed to place him on life support. After a while, it was finally determined that Keegan's only hope was a heart transplant, and it had to be performed soon.

On September 19, 2007, Keegan became the youngest and smallest heart transplant recipient in Texas and the smallest in the country. This miracle came in the form of an angel named Johnston. Johnston Lawrence Walker had been born in Houston, Texas, on the same day as Keegan. On the seventh day of his life, Johnston died of sudden infant death syndrome. It was heartbreaking to his family, yet even in their grief they courageously made the decision to donate Johnston's heart so that another child might live. Keegan was the blessed recipient of that tiny miraculous gift.

It has not been easy for Keegan and his family. He has had to deal with lots of other medical challenges, but he presently is twelve years old and is a happy, loving little boy. Gray and Maddie have since had a beautiful little girl, Audrey. And the Harrison family remains close friends with Johnston's family, Kevin and LaMonica Walker and their three younger children.

Keegan's medical issues meant that Maddie left her career as a successful attorney so that she could stay home and handle doctor appointments and the many issues that surround a child with health issues. And Gray works extra hard to provide for the family and to help with the challenges of being a parent of a child who has special needs. Together Gray and Maddie trust completely in God to guide them as they raise and support their family, and they are constantly assisting other families with children who have special health needs. They work tirelessly to get the word out about the gift of life through organ donation. They encourage people to give to COTA (Children's Organ Transplant Association) and have also formed their own organization "Ks for Keegan" as a platform to share how organ donation saved their son's life. They have seen God working in so many miraculous ways. When you know that you cannot make it through life on your own strength and expertise, then that is often when you have to let go and trust God to open doors for you, to lead you, and to provide all that is needed. Certainly, Gray and Maddie have watched as God has continued to direct their steps in the care of their dear son.

This precious family was given a gift—the gift of a child, the gift of medical expertise before and after he was born to save his life, and the precious gift of a tiny heart. They recognize all of the gifts they have been given, despite all of the difficulties they have gone through, and they work now to support other families and give them the gift of God's love any way that they possibly can.

Reflection Question:

What gifts have you been given and how are you giving back?

Divine Encounter 30

The Number of Hairs on Your Head

SOMETIMES WE CAN SEE God in the little details of life if we would only be willing to open our eyes. In 2009 I moved back to Texas from England. I got back on July 1 and my son, Kevin, and his adorable fiancée, Liz, were getting married on August 1. It felt like a whirlwind trying to get everything ready. We were going to have the wedding at Lovers Lane United Methodist Church where I had served prior to my going to England. I, along with my good friend, Dr. Stan Copeland, were officiating the service. My big prayer through all of this was, "Lord, please take care of all of the details." With just moving back to the United States, stepping into a new job, trying to find a place to live, buying a car, and getting ready for the wedding—I was overwhelmed. And I knew I was trying to juggle so many things that some would likely get dropped. I just kept praying, "Lord, handle the details, especially the details of this wedding."

We had a quick rehearsal on Friday evening so everyone would know where they were to stand and what they were supposed to do. There had been another event going on in the church on that evening, so we were not able to decorate the Fellowship Hall for the reception until Saturday morning even though the wedding was at 2:00 p.m. So, we rushed in that morning to decorate and then all the girls were supposed to get their hair done.

Someone I did not know was doing my hair. I was busy trying to make some notes about what I would say in the marriage ceremony, so I was not paying any attention to what he was doing. I knew he had pinned my hair up in the back and then coated it with lots of hair spray. When he said it was all finished, I looked in the mirror and immediately started crying.

I know it may sound so silly to most of you, but he had parted my hair on the wrong side. The wrong side! I always part it on the right side! He had parted it on the left side, and it just looked wrong. And all I could think was, "Heavenly Father, you were the one who was supposed to handle all the details! If you loved me, you would have at least gotten my hair right!"

The gentleman who was doing my hair was shocked by my hysterical crying and offered to change it, but there was not time. I would just have to wear my hair like this. My daughter, LeeRand, tried to calm me and tell me it looked great, yet I was so disappointed my hair would not be right on such a special day.

When we started the service, I remembered something about that sanctuary I had forgotten. You see, the Lovers Lane sanctuary is literally a stained glass box and the chancel area is like a wooden structure set inside it. There are some powerful air conditioning units that blow out a couple of vents on either side of the chancel. If you stand in front of the vents, it feels like you are standing in front of a jet airplane.

In fact, when I had served there as an associate pastor, we often laughed when I was the one to go down to the front of the chancel area to get the offering plates from the ushers and then take them to the altar at the back of the chancel area. Because every time I walked past the point where the vents were blowing, my long hair would all fly up in the air for about three steps until I passed the wind tunnel. Then it would come back down. Of course, it was not an issue for the guys on the staff, to them it just felt like a cool refreshing breeze. But you could always hear the congregation snicker when I went past it.

On the day of the wedding I had totally forgotten about the vents; they had not been turned on for the rehearsal the night before. Yet when the wedding began, Stan, the other minister, and I took our places in the center of the chancel, and at that moment I remembered the vents, and they were definitely blowing full blast. Thank goodness the gentleman who had fixed my hair had pinned it up and had parted it on the wrong side. I was standing near the vent on the left side so that the blowing air corresponded with the direction of the part. The direction of the blowing air was aerodynamically correct for my hair to remain in place since both the air and my hair were directed from the left to the right.

All I could do was stand there and smile and thank my Gracious God over and over in my head for taking care of the details and knowing what was best! If I had done it my way, my hair would have been down long and parted the way I usually did, and it would have been blowing all over the place, even if I had coated it with hair spray. I realized that not only does God know the number of hairs on our head,[1] but also knows to what side to comb them. If we open our eyes, we can often see God moving in the details of life.

Reflection Question:

Where have you recognized God in the details of your life?

---

1. Matt 10:30.

Divine Encounter 31

Being a Life Caddy

MY CHILDREN ARE THE greatest blessings in my life. When I think about them, I smile and ask, "Why me, Lord? Why was I so very blessed to have these two wonderful children?" They have both grown into amazing adults, and I love the fact that we can have deep spiritual conversations and share our lives together.

Even though I talked with my children each week while I was living in England, I still felt like I was missing out on being a part of their lives. Because of the six-hour time difference, it was not always the easiest to catch each other. And though we made a special effort on Sunday afternoons to visit by phone, I always felt that we missed that freedom of just being able to call anytime when an exciting event happened, or we needed someone with whom to laugh or cry.

It was great getting back to the States where I knew my children felt comfortable calling me at any time. One of the best calls came one day when my daughter, LeeRand, rang me up to ask if I would be her "Life Caddy."

"Your Life Caddy? What is a Life Caddy?" I just wanted to make sure I knew what I was committing to prior to saying yes.

She went on to explain that professional golfers have a caddy who is there to support them and when they are getting ready to make a critical shot, the golfer and the caddy confer beforehand discerning what is best. The caddy is the one who understands the hole and what the distance is, and they make a suggestion as to which club would be best to use in that situation. She went on to explain that the golfer is better at doing what they do because the caddy is there to guide them.

LeeRand told me she wanted me to be her Life Caddy and have the freedom to call me for advice and support as needed. Together we could discuss whatever she was facing and decide the best way for her to move forward. What a beautiful description, and I was honored that my precious daughter would value my opinion enough to ask me to be her Life Caddy!

That request was made several years ago, and every so often LeeRand calls and begins the conversation by saying, "I need my Life Caddy." And I know that we are about to enter into a serious conversation where I need to listen closely, pray, and then do my very best to advise her. I like the vision of walking side-by-side with my daughter and being there to support her when she needs my help. I pray that I will be a good Life Caddy, and that she can always count on me to guide her.

So, are there people in your life whom you can depend on to help guide you? Or maybe you are the one that others come to when they need help? Regardless of who is asking and who is being asked, hopefully time is taken to pray and ask for godly wisdom. We see things from a very human perspective, yet God's view encompasses so much more. God's thoughts and ways are so much higher than ours.[1]

Actually, when you think about it, there may be wise people in our lives who can help advise us, but the Holy Spirit is the ultimate Life Caddy. God knows all things and God's Spirit is always with us, so what a perfect one to guide us. Just think, if we would take time to listen to the Holy Spirit, we really could play this game of life so much better!

Reflection Question:

Who do you depend on to guide you?

1. Isa 55:8–9.

Divine Encounter 32

Hearing God's Voice

I LOVE HEARING HOW different people have received divine guidance from God's voice. Certainly, the Lord God Almighty can speak to us in a variety of ways—through Scripture or prayer, an audible voice or that sense of knowing or whisper, through nature, or through other people, or really however God would like to share knowledge with us. The Lord definitely has the power and it is obvious from the Bible that God enjoys doing it in a variety of ways—even speaking through a burning bush,[1] a floating hand writing on the wall of the palace,[2] and my favorite—a talking donkey.[3]

My dear friend Norma Stachura has a wonderful testimony of how God spoke to her. To give you a little background, Norma and I met when I moved back to the United States and was appointed to serve at First Church in Carrollton as an associate pastor. She was gracious enough to reach out to me when I first moved there and did not really know anyone. She and another friend had invited me to lunch, and it was a great opportunity for us to talk about where we had seen God working in our lives. Norma and I became accountability partners in helping each other grow in our faith.

The season of Lent is the forty days (not counting Sundays) that lead up to Easter. It is a special time in the Christian calendar where you are trying to go even deeper in your relationship with God. Often Christians will decide to give up something during that time (like chocolate, or TV, or something that might be a distraction) or they may instead plan to do something extra during that season (like an extra Bible study, or a special prayer time). The idea is to do something that changes up your routine so that you are more sensitive and aware of God. During Lent one year, Norma and I decided that we would do a twenty-one-day cleanse as a way of fasting and trying to hear the Lord better. It was the type of fast/detox where you

1. Exod 3:2–6.
2. Dan 5:5.
3. Num 22:28–30.

126

normally eat vegetables, but you would also have protein shakes that you mixed with bananas and other fruit.

That was the year that two of our friends, John and Sharmy McDonald, really felt that God had placed on their heart to have a prayer room during Holy Week and for our church to pray around the clock 24/7 from Palm Sunday until Easter. Part of the inspiration came from hearing about Count Zinzendorf.

I had read that Count Zinzendorf had a passionate love for Jesus Christ and out of that love came a disciplined life of prayer. In 1727, Count Zinzendorf's small church in Hernhunt, Germany, felt God's call to begin "Hourly Intercession." The congregation of this 150-member church began praying twenty-four hours a day every single day with a relay of prayers by brothers and sisters. "Prayer without ceasing was made to God for all the work and wants of His church." This prayer vigil was every single day for twenty-four hours a day and lasted for one hundred years. Through their devotion to God and discipline of prayer, this small church sent out more missionaries throughout the entire world than all the missionary boards put together. It was through the influence of some of these Moravian missionaries that the lives of John and Charles Wesley were turned around and ultimately led to the development of the Methodist denomination.

John and Sharmy took our existing prayer room and really made it special for Holy Week. It was a great room in which to pray before, but they wanted to do something powerful for that time period. They covered the walls with black construction paper and had chalk available so that people could write scripture or prayers on the wall. They brought in a really large cross and a kneeler and soft music and candles. It just changed the atmosphere and ambiance of the room so that it felt even more sacred than usual. Then they put together a chart for every hour of the week and it was made available so that people could sign up for an hour-long slot and reserve their time before Holy Week even began.

The church was excited about participating in the around-the-clock prayers. Most of the slots were just individuals, but in some cases, it was couples or a family that might reserve a slot. Before Palm Sunday came almost all of the slots were taken except for a few in the late night / early morning.

Norma had signed up for one of the nighttime slots. To be honest, she was not really feeling that well and had seemed to be getting worse the last few weeks. No one would have blamed her for just not showing up in the middle of the night to pray for an hour, but Norma had put her name on the chart and committed to herself and to her church—and more than that, to God—that she would be praying during her time slot. You have to know

Norma; she is probably one of the most loyal and hardworking individuals that I know. Even in times when she is struggling with her health or her own personal challenges, she still will put in a tremendous amount of time to do her job or go above and beyond to help someone else. So, she definitely was going to be there to pray.

When she arrived to pray, she noticed that the slot right after her was one of the few that had been left empty, which meant that no one would be knocking on the prayer room door after just an hour. Instead, it would be two hours before the next person arrived in the dark to continue the prayer time. She decided right then she would be responsible for and take advantage of the second hour as well as her original commitment.

Norma recognizes how precious it is to pray and spend time with the Lord, so she began praying for our church and all the ministries, for our city and state, for our nation and our world. As it got close to the end of the second hour and she had been faithfully pouring out her heart to the Lord in intercession for everything else, she finally turned her prayers to her own needs. She humbly placed before the Lord her own health, and the fact that it seemed like she was getting sicker and sicker as time went on. She didn't know what was going on with her body, but she just had not felt well for the last few weeks and it seemed to be getting worse. She asked for God's healing touch and that he might give her wisdom as to what she should do to improve her health so that she could use her strength to serve.

At that moment she heard God's audible voice and one word . . . "Bananas." That's it! Just one word! We often think how great it would be for God to give us a scripture or a quote that we can cross-stitch on a pillow or make into a bumper sticker. But all God gave Norma that night was—"Bananas."

As strange as it seems, that one word was exactly what she needed. You see, Norma never knew it before then, but she was allergic to bananas. In doing the twenty-one-day cleanse she had not been eating much more than vegetables and the shakes. And as she got to feeling worse, she decided it was just because she was not getting enough calories, so she had increased the number of shakes that she was drinking every day. And since each shake was made with bananas, she was slowly making herself even more ill. Thank goodness God said bananas to her because it made her go back and try to figure out why that was the message that was given to her. As soon as she stopped eating bananas, then she started feeling much better.

To me this is just one more example of God loving us so very much that the Lord is willing to be intimately involved in our daily lives. How glorious it is that when Norma heard God's voice it was to give her one word that on the surface seemed like a strange message yet had a powerful impact on her health and life.

I really do believe that God is speaking to us all the time, but too often we are too busy to listen. Or maybe we do hear the Lord, and because the message is not what we are expecting . . . then we just ignore God's words. Are you listening?

Reflection Question:

In what ways has God warned you?

Strangely Warmed

WHAT I HAVE LEARNED to believe without a doubt is that God is always with us and God always hears our prayers. Both of these assurances are constantly being revealed in our daily lives. It often requires open eyes to see what is going on and having a faith in the Lord.

I know there are instances when people have seen God show up in their lives in those big crisis times, but I think one of the things that is so comforting to me is that the Lord even cares about the little events and things in our lives. Sometimes God demonstrates love for us in the details and tiny desires. It can be some small unimportant request, and yet when God is revealed, it feels like a precious kiss on the cheek that says, "I just wanted you to know that I love you and even the random requests in your life are important to me . . . because you are important to me."

One of the fun examples of this began when I was in England. I purchased a car while I was over there. It was a baby blue Rover and two of the greatest things about it were that it had an automatic transmission (most cars in the UK are manual shift), and it had seat warmers. Seat warmers! Isn't that exciting. I had never even heard of cars where in addition to turning on the general heat in the car, you could also turn on a little heater actually built into the car seat, and you could warm your backside. Since I am always cold, I thought this was the most magnificent invention ever. I used it year-round while in the UK. And it broke my heart when I left England and had to leave my car behind.

When I arrived back in Texas in July of 2009, the last thing I was thinking about was turning on a heater. I arrived in town without a car or a place to live. The very first day that I flew to Dallas, I was notified that a sweet couple from First Church, Carrollton, Dan and Carol McCann, had a car that they were offering for me to drive the next three months. It was a fabulous car and such a blessing to use while I was getting settled. But ultimately, I needed to find a car that I could purchase and keep. I did some shopping for used cars and found a Nissan Maxima that I liked and purchased it.

Then one day my senior pastor, Dr. Richard Dunagin, bought himself a new car. It was a cute little red sports car with all the bells and whistles. When the staff was looking at it to see all the features, one of the things that he pointed out was that it had seat warmers. All of a sudden, I really missed my car in England and my very own seat warmers. My new (used) car was OK, but it was lacking in the seat heat area. I hate to admit it, but I was jealous that his car had seat warmers and mine did not.

One of the Ten Commandments is that "you shall not covet."[1] I was really trying hard not to covet or lust after those fancy cars that had this ingenious invention. But it became increasingly difficult, especially one very cold winter night when I had stayed at the church office until almost midnight and by the time I came out, it was below freezing and sleeting. I got into my really cold car and cranked up the heater hoping that it would warm up fast, and that is when I really started wishing for seat warmers. I started talking to God on my drive home about how thankful I was that I had a car that started in this ridiculously cold weather, but I also mentioned how it would have been a really special blessing if there were seat warmers in my car. I kid you not, as I was praying and talking to God, I literally started feeling my backside getting warmer. I thought I was hallucinating at first. Was this just my imagination? It really did feel like it was getting hot! I just giggled and kept talking to God and was just amazed at how miraculously my prayer had been answered.

I had been exhausted when I left the office, but by the time I got home I was so thrilled about my answered prayer that I could barely sleep. The next morning, I got up and headed to the office and before I got in the car, I had convinced myself that the warm event from the night before was probably just one of those one-time God-moments. Even though it was still really cold outside, I could not imagine that God would once again heat up the seat. But what do you know, as I was driving to the office talking to God, it happened once again—I literally could feel my seat getting warmer and warmer. God is so good! Amen!

By the time I got to the office, I was giggly and excited about God answering my prayer a second time and heating up my seat. Since I had felt guilty about lusting after Richard's seat warmers, I could not wait to go in to tell him about God's gift to me. I enthusiastically told him the story about what had happened both the night before and that morning. Richard

---

1. Exod 20:17.

just looked at me and with his witty sense of humor said, "Let me get this straight, are you telling me that your *seat was strangely warmed*"?

Hearing those words, we both started laughing. If you are a Methodist and are familiar with church history, you will remember that John Wesley had a life-changing moment when he really knew that God loved him, and he wrote in his diary that in that instant his "heart was strangely warmed." I guess in my God-moment the experience was just as loving and warming, but in a different location.

So how do you explain such a wonderful warming God experience? Actually, I could not explain it for several months. It did not happen again, even though there were other cold days, and I was still talking to God while driving. It was as if God had answered my prayers that night and the next morning and then had decided to not give me a warm car seat anymore.

Then one day I jumped in the car to head somewhere and I placed my notebook and purse right next to me on the console (instead of in the passenger seat). When I did, I heard a click. I wondered what I had done and began examining the console closer. What I discovered was that there were two little flip switches that were under the middle armrest. I had never noticed them before because of their positioning. But as I lifted up the armrest and looked closer, I realized that they were switches for seat warmers for both the driver's seat and the passenger's seat. Oh, my goodness! My car did have seat warmers, and I had never known it. Apparently, that freezing night when I had gotten into the car, I must have placed my purse in such a way that it hit the switch for the seat warmer. As I drove home talking to God, it was slowly getting warmer and the timing was perfect for an answered prayer.

You know, someone told me once that some miracles are actually everyday events that have a very rational explanation, but what makes them miraculous is their perfect timing. For example, in Matthew 17:24–27 Jesus tells Peter to go fishing and in the first fish he would catch there would be a four-drachma coin to pay the taxes. A fisherman in Israel explained to me that one of the main fishes in Lake Tiberias (also known as the Sea of Galilee) was a bottom feeder, and it would be attracted to shiny things so there is a possibility that it would swallow a coin. So, the miracle would not be that there was a coin in the fish, but that at that exact instant that would be the very fish that Peter would catch, and that it would be the very amount needed to pay the taxes.

I guess that is how I feel about the miracle of when my "seat was strangely warmed." Since I never knew that I had that extra feature in my automobile, the blessing from God is that the Lord chose to demonstrate it to me at the very moment when I was asking for it. I know it is a silly little thing, but it really does feel like a precious kiss from God

Reflection Question:

What miracles has God demonstrated to you?

Praying for Rain

ONE BEAUTIFUL DAY, AROUND the beginning of 2014, my son, Kevin, called and asked if he and his wife, Liz, could come over to the house to talk. Of course! I always love having them, especially since they would be bringing my only grandchild, London. He was about nineteen months old by this time and toddling all over the place. As soon as they walked in the door, I greeted Kevin and Liz, but then was focused on holding and playing with London. It took me a while to realize his little T-shirt he was wearing proclaimed, "I'm going to be a big brother."

"How wonderful!" I was delighted. They were giddy with excitement and said they had so much to tell me. We sat down as they began to unfold what was a much bigger revelation than just the fact that they were expecting. They began sharing about all of the God-things that had been going on around this pregnancy.

Liz explained that mid-December Kevin was anxious to start trying to have a second child, but she was worried and really fearful it was too soon. London was still small, she had not totally gotten where she wanted her body to be from the first pregnancy, and financially she wasn't sure they were in the right place to add to their family and so she was feeling very nervous about it. But Kevin was so excited about the idea of growing the family that Liz just prayed and asked God if it was really the right time. She stated that immediately it was as if this peace flowed over her, and she was no longer fearful of going ahead with another child. She felt it was God's way of saying, "Just let go and trust me." So, with that godly comfort she relaxed and knew it was the right time. The moment she surrendered to the idea of having another child, then she had a vision from God. She tried to explain what it was like—sort of like a flash of information where she saw four things listed, but it wasn't a list. It was more like a stack of four pieces of information in order. The four statements were: "You are conceiving. It's a girl. Her name is Rain. September 13."

Oh, my goodness! They said I was the first person they had told, but that there had been other things that had happened which seemed to confirm it. The next morning following the vision when London woke up one of the first things he did was pat Liz on the stomach as she held him and said, "Baby, baby." He had never even said "baby" before, and they were shocked he would do such a thing.

Maybe they were really attuned to listening at this point, but they heard other hints they thought had to do with Rain being on her way. They shared about when they had gone to see Kevin's dad and stepmom, and his dad commented in casual conversation about hearing a weatherman on TV make the statement it was a 100 percent chance of rain. He noted he had heard high percentages of rain or a particular weather event predicted, but he could not remember a weatherperson ever stating something was a 100 percent. After all, it was just a prediction, not something for sure. Kevin and Liz just looked at each other. And his wife kept singing a little tune while they were there, and the tune was "Singing in the Rain." Neither Kevin nor Liz had mentioned anything about Rain at that point, so they just held it in their hearts that maybe God was confirming it.

They both felt they had spiritual confirmation this child was coming, but they did not have earthly confirmation. It had only been a couple of weeks, but Liz wanted to go ahead and take one of the pregnancy tests to see if it showed anything. Kevin tried to tell her it was still too early to tell, but she said she just wanted to see. Sure enough, there was a faint line showing the test was positive. She was pregnant. Then later when she had a sonogram, it showed that it definitely was a girl. So, it was decided that absolutely her name would be Rain. We all began to pray for Rain. I could not wait for this tiny little girl to show up.

Not long after that, I was offered an opportunity to go to a church in Henrietta, Texas. It was a couple of hours northwest of Dallas. I went for the "seating" (as it is called in the United Methodist Church) with the district superintendent and the church's PPRC (Pastor Parish Relations Committee). A seating is a meeting where the pastor, who the bishop is appointing to the church, is taken to the new church and is introduced to a committee representing the church. It is an opportunity for the pastor to see the church, and the church to have a preliminary meeting with the pastor. I immediately fell in love with the people at Henrietta FUMC. They were all so gracious and welcoming.

When they asked about my family, I told them about my amazing daughter, LeeRand, who lived in Houston, and that I had a wonderful son and daughter-in-law, Kevin and Liz, and my adorable grandson, London. I also alerted them that my new granddaughter was due in the middle of

September. Several of the members spoke up and quickly let me know that I could not have a grandchild on the third weekend in September. What? I did not know the job came with such restrictions. They laughed and went on to tell me that Pioneer Reunion was the third weekend every September and that it had been going on for eighty-three years. It consists of rodeos and parades and is always an amazing time for the city. They were all excited about it. I laughed and said that I would let my daughter-in-law, Liz, know to either have the baby before or after that weekend. (By the way, I did make a note to myself to check to see when September 13 was that year and realized it was the second weekend in September. If God really did intend for her to be born on that date, then it would not be a conflict. I figured God is big enough to handle dates for everything and could direct where I needed to be at the right time.)

I had visited the new church and met the PPRC in the middle of March but would not take over as pastor until July 1. In the meantime, I wanted to make sure that I was praying for the church and the community. In order to really cover someone or some place in prayer, you need to know everything you can about them. So, I started studying up on the area and praying through the church directory.

One of the big prayer concerns in that area was rain. They desperately needed rain. Someone told me that it had been about five years of drought. That is difficult in any area, but this was ranching country and in order for many of the ranches to continue in business, they must have rain. So, I started praying for rain in this part of Texas. By the way, the day that I moved into the parsonage in Henrietta it finally started to rain, and we had a couple of inches. Everyone was excited to get that amount, but the ranches definitely needed more. So, we kept praying for rain.

As I started getting settled in the house and began getting involved in the community, I noticed that everywhere people had "Pray for Rain" signs in their yards, in windows, and on bulletin boards. Even the bank in Byers, a little town in Clay County not far from Henrietta, had a scrolling sign that said, "Pray for rain."

During that time, I was praying for Rain (my granddaughter), and then when it came time to pray for my community and all the area, I would pray for rain for the land. One day, while praying, I just laughed at the irony of it all. "Lord, how about if I just pray for 'Rain' and you'll know that includes both my precious granddaughter as well as the moisture falling to the ground!" After that, when I ran around town and saw all of the signs, I just smiled to myself and thought how cool it was that everyone was praying for my granddaughter.

September came, and it was getting close to both Rain's birth date, as well as Pioneer Reunion. It was going to be interesting to see when she would be born.

As it was getting closer to the due date, Kevin and Liz happened to be watching the Christian movie *Facing the Giants*. It is a movie about a high-school football coach who is having a really tough time in his life. There is a scene in the movie where a man from the community comes to visit the coach and give him an encouraging word about trusting God. He tells the coach a story that he heard about two farmers who desperately needed rain. Both prayed for rain, but only one of them went out and prepared his field to receive it. And then he asked, "Which one do you think trusted God to send the rain?" The coach answered, "Well, the one who prepared his fields for it." And the man asked, "Which one are you?"

That scene touched Liz and Kevin deeply. God had given them so many signs around this pregnancy. Everything that God had said so far had come true. They had conceived a child, it was a girl, and they were certainly planning on naming her Rain just as God had said. So, the only part that was in question was the date of her birth. They realized if they really did trust God they would continue to move forward with preparations and plans for what God had told them regarding when Rain would be born.

Actually, there had been some question of the due date from the doctor. The doctor had given two dates, the 11th and the 17th. Because Liz has high-risk pregnancies, it was suggested that they go ahead and do a C-section early, so it was scheduled for the 10th. Liz was tired of being pregnant and was really ready to have this baby. But as Kevin and Liz talked about it, Kevin pointed out that God had given the date of the 13th, and so he really wanted to at least wait until then. On the other hand, God had stated the date "September 13," but in the vision he did not say that was her birth date. They had assumed that was what that date meant in relationship to the other three pieces of information that were "stacked." Would she really be born on that date?

They had shared with family and friends about the vision and how God had been showing up in this pregnancy, but they had not told their doctor. They decided they should share with him. After hearing everything, the doctor was definitely willing to try to reschedule the C-section to the 13th, but when he checked, it was a Saturday and he would be gone on a trip with his family. Kevin and Liz decided to "prepare their fields" in expectation that God would do it on the date he had said. They scheduled the C-section for the 15th trusting that if God wanted to bring her sooner, he could work out all the details to make sure everything was covered.

On the 12th, Kevin called me. The next day was Saturday, and he asked if I would mind coming and spending the day with Liz. He had to work that day, but since the 13th was the original date that God had given, they would feel a little better if someone was with Liz. I said I would be delighted to come.

The next morning was the 13th and when Liz woke around 4:30 a.m. she said she had a weird feeling. She wasn't sure she was really in labor; it just felt different. I arrived in Arlington at their apartment, and Liz and I decided we would go shopping and to eat and maybe a movie. We just thought it would be fun to do things together . . . and we would see if anyone else decided to show up. We had a great time running all over the place and doing things. Throughout the day she had a few pains, but certainly not consistent ones, so we dismissed it.

Since they had shared their witness of what God had been doing the past several months around this pregnancy, then there were a lot of other people wondering if September 13 would be the day that Rain really showed up. They kept texting Liz throughout the day to check on her. When it got to be evening, it seemed like the contractions were a little more often and harder. We decided to go to the hospital just to check it out. We called Kevin to let him know. From the time they started monitoring her, the contractions tripled in one hour. The nurses started calling the doctor on call to let her know the baby was coming. The new doctor rushed to the hospital to go ahead and perform the C-section. The nurses and this doctor did not know anything about the vision or the September 13 date, and yet they were rushing around saying they needed to get the baby out by midnight.

Brooklyn Rain Green was born at 10:30 p.m. on September 13, 2014 (just as God had said). They liked the name Brooklyn since London was already named after a city, but since God said her name was Rain, then that would definitely be what they called her. Mother and baby were both doing great, thanks to all of the prayers.

This entire experience has been an incredible witness to so many people who heard beforehand about the vision and then saw it all come true when this new life made her timely entrance into this world. We wonder what God has in store for this precious little girl named Rain. It is going to be fun watching to see how the Lord uses her.

And by the way, yes, Henrietta and Clay County got lots of rain that fall. God does answer prayers!

Reflection Question:

How have you seen God direct your future?

Divine Encounter 35

God's Will and God's Timing

SOMETIMES YOU FEEL LIKE you know what God is saying for the future and what he is guiding you to do, and yet it may be that you continue to meet opposition so that you wonder if you heard the Lord correctly. It can seem at those times as if God has given us visions or desires for certain things, but we can't seem to get any closer to achieving that goal to which we feel the Lord is calling us. Maybe the true prize is not in achieving the goal, but primarily in the journey.

Some people know exactly what they want to be when they "grow up" and they can shoot for that goal from an early age. And then there are lots of others who bounce around considering different options trying to figure out what is right for them. My son, Kevin, considered a few different options. When he was young and Michael Jordan was his hero, he considered pro-basketball. But like a lot of other young men, he realized that maybe that wasn't the most realistic goal. He loves music and has a real ear for it and has a degree in music composition. But he realized when he married that maybe he needed to find a steady job that could provide a stable income to meet their financial needs.

At some point as a young adult, the idea of becoming a firefighter captured his heart. And after he set his sights on the opportunity to serve others in that arena then nothing could distract him from that goal. Of course, the fact that he married into a family of firemen probably helped fan those flames of desire. From the time that Kevin first met Liz, his future wife, she had shared wonderful stories about growing up with her dad as a fireman. Her dad, Bob, was a lieutenant for the Arlington Fire Department and her older brother, Rob, would later be the chief of a local fire department. Fighting fire was in their DNA.

Kevin and Liz set their sights early in their marriage on the goal of his becoming a firefighter. I say they set "their sights" because I realize now that becoming a firefighter is really a family affair. It should be true in all careers and marriages that the couple is linked together in support for each other, but maybe that is even truer in the case of first responders.

For the rest of our family, I'm not sure we had any idea of what it took to become a firefighter. When Kevin decided that was what he wanted to pursue, then as a mother I was both proud and concerned. I liked the idea of him being a hero and knew that he would look good in a uniform, but as his mother I was not overly excited about him being in dangerous situations. Yet I knew deep down that he had the courage and compassion to do whatever it took to rescue others and save lives.

But just knowing that is what you want to become does not mean that it is always easy to get to that point. I had no concept for how competitive it is to become a firefighter. I guess I figured it was like a lot of other job opportunities; you put in an application and go after the job.

It seems like the first one he applied for was the Fort Worth Fire Department in 2011. The first step of the process is to take a written exam. I remember his going to the Fort Worth Convention Center for the exam. That should tell you something about how many applicants take the test if they have to hold it in the Convention Center. There were several thousand who were there to apply and take that first test. And oh, by the way, they might ultimately hire less than ten firefighters, so obviously this was just the first step and the competition was tight. You had to be in the top one hundred to go on to the next step of the process. Unfortunately, that time he was not in that top group.

Kevin started studying passionately so that the next time he applied at a department he would do better. Each fire department may only hire once a year, so if you do not get hired, then you have to wait until the next year. And different departments had different requirements. There are multiple steps to whittling the huge number of applicants down to the small number that a fire department will ultimately hire. That should make us as the public feel safer knowing there are such high standards, but for those going through the process it can be extremely challenging.

Often it begins with a difficult written test that not only tests knowledge but can also test psychologically if you are the right personality for the job. Only those scoring in the very top percentile are invited to continue the process. Then the next testing may focus on physical strength and endurance, making the candidates run a mile or two within a certain time limit. The following tests may be other physical challenges such as dragging hoses, or climbing ladders or stairs while carrying a dummy, or crawling through a tiny space while holding on to a weight, or any number of difficult activities which demonstrate strength and how quickly you can respond. Passing the physical agility portion opens the opportunity to go through other reviews and exams that include extensive packets to be completed and detailed background checks and psychological exams and several levels of interviews. Needless to say, there are lots of levels and hoops and steps of the process in which at any point you can be told either that you continue in the process or that you are eliminated.

We watched for several years as Kevin would continue over and over to pursue this dream. He felt like this was where God was calling him to serve and so he was persistent in continuing. But I have to tell you, it was like a roller coaster for Kevin and Liz and all of us. We would pray and encourage him each step of the way, and I know as difficult as it was to be on the outside watching, that it had to be even more difficult for him. We would get excited with each step of the process in the various fire departments. He would go take the test or particular step in the process, and we would wait with excitement for the results. We would celebrate for him with each positive result and cry a little with each setback.

The whole time he was applying, he was trying to put himself in the best position for the next opportunity. He realized it would help if he went to EMT (Emergency Medical Training) school, so while he was working full-time at another job during the day, he attended EMT at night. By then they had their first child so that made it even more of a challenge.

Kevin had various jobs throughout this process, but he knew that his ultimate goal was to be a firefighter, so he was willing to do whatever needed to be done. Twice that meant quitting his job to go full-time to school, once for attending the fire academy, and once for paramedic school. In many cases, if you secure a position with a fire department, they will cover your educational expenses for additional schooling while you are on salary. Kevin knew that it would increase his opportunities to be a viable candidate if he went ahead and took those classes on his own, so he was willing to sacrifice to be the very best he could be.

There were several times when Kevin would get to the very last step, the chief's interview, or even be told that he had one of the positions, only to find out that something had changed or there was a delay in hiring. It was heartbreaking to watch as Kevin and Liz would get so excited about the opportunities for a job where he could serve in such a way, only to have it slip away at the last moment.

Kevin started his job search in 2011 and finally in 2016 he was hired as a firefighter with the Richardson Fire Department. It took over five years of constantly applying and studying and trying to get on with a department to become a firefighter. In that time, he was denied at least twenty times.

I can honestly say that as a parent, often the most painful things in life are not what happens to us, but those disappointments that happen to our children. We would love to protect them and for life to always work out for them, but sometimes all we can do is circle them in prayer and stand on the sidelines to support them.

So, you may be wondering where in the world I saw God as my son continually went through rejections in trying to become a firefighter? Through Kevin's struggle, I felt God present in him throughout his unmitigated faith that he would fulfill his life purpose as a firefighter. I witnessed how Kevin depended on God for strength and the courage to go on. And I saw how Kevin and Liz grew in faith as they totally depended on God to provide for their family during this time. They would pray together and study Scripture together and write notes and post them all over the house as an encouragement that God was with them every step of the way. Their family grew from one child to three children during those years as Kevin continued to pursue what he felt God had directed as his goal. He truly felt it was God's will for him to become a firefighter, and so he had to trust that in God's perfect timing it would all work out.

It reminds me of a story of a man God instructs to go out and push against a heavy stone. The man goes to push on it and no matter how hard he tries, he cannot budge the stone. He continues to push against the stone every single day giving it his very best effort. Finally, after months of pushing and never seeing any progress, the man complains to God that he is giving up because he cannot do what God had instructed him to do. He explained that he had pushed hard all this time and never moved the stone a single inch. God then reminded him that he never told him to move the stone. He just told him to push against it and that was exactly what the man had done. And God told him to look at his muscles and how he had built up the strength in his arms and legs and back from constantly pushing. The intent was to build him up—not move the stone.

Looking back, I can see that same story in Kevin. Granted, God did finally open the door so Kevin could become a firefighter for one of the very best fire departments in the area. And now he has a wonderful job he really enjoys, and it is a great way to support his sweet family. But even more than that, I can see how much growth has been made through the years—growth in character, and faith, and appreciation of the little things in life, and a strong marriage.

Kevin probably says it best: "The biggest lesson for me was God's will for my life was clear, but God's timing was not. I look at my life and who I was when I started this journey and I see a kid who had a lot to learn. Now, five years, three kids, countless number of tests, applications, physical agility tests, and interviews later, I see that God needed a better servant to fulfill his will. He needed to mold me into a man with more grace, patience, and strength. I know he's not done with me, but I'm glad to be moving to the next chapter."

Maybe this is a good lesson for all of us. Sometimes God does not immediately give us what we want or think we need, because the Lord is still doing things to make us better equipped to handle the blessings that are in store for us. I truly believe in God's timing, and sometimes we just need to continue on the path on which we feel God is leading us as we trust that ultimately the Lord's will . . . will be done.

Reflection Question:

What areas of your life do you need to trust to God?

Divine Encounter 36

Prayer Partners

I CONTINUE TO BE awed by the power of prayer. I truly believe that prayer is one of the most amazing vehicles we have to get closer to God, and yet I see so many Christians who do not seem to utilize it. My desire is to constantly be in prayer and to help others grow in their prayer life (and not just when they are riding with me in a car while I am driving in another country).

Since the primary role that I believe God has called me to do is to preach, I always want to make sure that my sermons are covered in lots of prayer. That means that each week I try to start out by having a "God-day" where I attempt to spend a lot of time in prayer. I certainly pray for all of the people in the church and everyone for whom I know something particular is going on in their lives, but also a big part of my God-day is to begin my preparation for the sermon in lots of prayer. That is often a key time to hear from God on insights of what needs to be included in the upcoming sermon.

My running time each morning is also a key time for me to pray. I always try to run throughout the areas where I live so that I can pray for my neighbors, local businesses, and the entire community. Recently I lived in the small town of Henrietta, Texas. After living there for a short time, everyone seemed to know that I would particularly set my route for the early morning runs so that I could pass the house of someone who was having a birthday or had a need where they might could use an extra prayer or blessing. Sometimes I would even get a call or a comment from someone suggesting a home that I should run past so that I could pray for a particular need or issue. Also, my combination of running while praying fosters a mind-set that gives me greater clarity in facing the issues that arise daily.

In addition to pouring out my prayers for others and lifting up issues within the church, I also know it is important for me to have believers praying for me. On my birthday, March 10, 2013, God gave me a wonderful gift. It was the idea to contact three or four individuals or families each week and ask them to be in prayer for me for that particular week. I usually make contact on Monday so they can be praying all week long. I know I will be working on the sermon throughout the week and if they can be praying for me, then it seems to make such a huge difference. I request they pray that my ears will be open so I can hear clearly from God what needs to be preached on the upcoming Sunday. I know the only way my words will have any value is if those words are from God. If it is just me up there spouting my own thoughts, then it is really a waste of everyone's time. So, it is to their advantage and mine for them to be praying for me throughout the week. I ask their prayers for the sermon, but also for the entire service so every element of the worship time is covered in prayer.

I have also found that those individuals and families I have asked to pray during that week feel more connected to the service and sermon. They recognize they are partly responsible for what does or does not go on based on their faithfulness in prayer. There are some of my precious congregation who if it has been their week to pray will come up to me after the service and say something like, "We did a good job on that one this week." They recognize they truly were a part of the sermon/service preparation process and the outcome was worthwhile.

The plan is not only for my prayer partners for that particular week to be circling me in lots of prayer, but also that I am spending extra time making sure I am covering them. When I email them at the first of the week to be my prayer partners and to pray for all areas of the service, I also ask what things they would like for me to be lifting to the Lord on their behalf. Most of them will give me a list of special requests to pray about. It helps me to better know what is going on in their lives and how I can best support them as their pastor. And though I try to pray for my entire congregation by name every week, I make sure those prayer partners are particularly circled and covered in lots and lots of prayer.

God has given us this incredible gift of prayer so we can communicate with the Lord and have a closer relationship. It is also our privilege to pray for others and help draw them closer to the Lord as well. It is a gift—a gift that is intended to be opened and used. And when we join our hearts and our prayers together, then there is even more unity and power as we honor the Lord together.

Reflection Question:

How is God calling you to strengthen your prayer life?

Sometimes You Just Have to Dance

WHEN MY GRANDSON, LONDON, turned five years old it meant he was old enough to come to Mimi's house for the week and go to Vacation Bible School. (For my English friends, VBS is usually a week of church events for children from about five years old until eleven years old, which includes Bible stories, singing, crafts, games, science projects, and lots of fun.)

I was really excited to have him at my home for the week and for him to be able to participate in VBS, but it also meant a lot of extra distraction, in an already busy week. Like most folks, I seem to have a lot going on each week with just the regular things in the community and the various weekly activities of the church. There never seems to be enough time to get everything done the way I would like. But then if you add on a hundred extra children and staff running around the church every day and trying to keep up with an inquisitive five-year-old starting early in the morning until the evening, then things seem more than a little hectic.

I really was enjoying it, but it was throwing my routine off. My routine included my early morning runs, prayer time, and juicing. Even my sleep routine was disrupted with the addition of a little person slipping into my bed in the middle of the night. Of course, this was delightful, but the next day I felt a little off kilter.

One of the mornings toward the end of the week, I was hurrying, trying to get ready so we could get next door to the church for the beginning of VBS. London was so precious. He had already dressed himself, was eating the breakfast I had set out for him and was watching a movie. As I rushed around like a chicken with its head cut off, London came into my bathroom to tell me something. I said I needed to get ready and tried to send him back to the other room. He could tell I was preoccupied and busy, so he grabbed both of my hands and said, "Mimi!" I stopped and looked at him. With those big, beautiful, brown eyes and angelic face, he looked up at me and said, "Sometimes you just have to stop and dance." And there in my bathroom he turned me around in a complete circle. Then he smiled and ran back into the other room, leaving me just standing there.

Wow! He was right. From the lips of a five-year-old! Sometimes you do just have to stop whatever you are doing and instead—dance! I realized in that moment that I had so much for which to be thankful. One of my greatest blessings is certainly that precious little grandson. I realized that I was letting life slip away. I was so busy trying to handle things, I was missing the true dance and joy of life.

It was a good wake-up call for me to be reminded that life is too precious just to be rushing through it without taking time to see what God is doing all around us. We need to enjoy family, friends, and the thrill of living. I am hoping from this point on I may be able to listen more for the rhythm of life, enjoy people, and celebrate the many opportunities . . . to just dance.

Reflection Question:

How is God reminding you to recognize joy?

Experiences Around the World

Divine Encounter 38

An Icy Volcano

GOD HAS BLESSED ME with amazing friends! I have them in all areas of my life. But some of my most adventurous friends are Carol Gradziel, Jan Pasternak, and Holly Montalbano. We all met in WBSN (Women's Business Support Network), a networking organization in Houston during the 1980s and 1990s. It was an incredible group of businesswomen who got together at the Ritz Carlton Hotel at 6:30 a.m. every Thursday morning to support and encourage each other in our various businesses. I am so blessed with so many wonderful friendships from that group. Carol, Jan, and Holly were some of the crazier ones who loved to go and do exciting things.

We started running races together—5Ks, 10Ks, half-marathons, and even marathons. We also were into bike riding and did the MS-150 together for a few years. Of course, there were also the easier things around town like meals, movies, and fun times just sitting around talking.

I think Carol was the one who started the birthday trips. She had a big one coming up and she wanted to go run a marathon. I had run several by that point and told her I would be glad to go with her, as long as it was somewhere in the United States. She came back and said she had actually decided on a half-marathon. Great! I'm in. And then she told me it was a half-marathon running up Pikes Peak. (By the way, Pikes Peak is 14,114 feet high!) What a way to celebrate! It was tough, but a great accomplishment.

I can't remember whose birthday it was when we decided to ride bicycles across Yellowstone and the Grand Tetons and camp as we went across. We also did some kayaking on that fun trip. Holly particularly liked the hot tub when we finally reached Jackson Hole, Wyoming. She said that when she planned her next trip it would be a weeklong spa.

Jan was the next one to have a special birthday (we decided we would only do the big trips for the five- and ten-year birthdays). She chose Ecuador and to work at an orphanage for a week. (She has such a big heart!) Carol and Holly were able to go with her on her big trip, but her birthday

151

was in April and by that time I was in seminary and it was finals week, so I had to live vicariously through their pictures and great stories.

I think I was next, and I opted for riding bicycles across Portugal. Except instead of camping we stayed in five-star hotels. Holly really thought the hotels were a great idea.

Then finally it was Holly's birthday trip. She had thought about it and planned for years. We expected the weeklong spa or taking it easy on a beach, but she surprised us. It was a couple of weeks in the mountains of Patagonia. We would fly into Argentina and then make our way across to Chile. The trip included horseback riding and biking and the high point was an opportunity to climb an ice-covered volcano. That was the part Holly was most excited about. She had certainly surprised us with her choice of trip. It was a glorious time together.

Holly was right; by far the greatest part was climbing Villarrica Volcano! And it is where I learned some amazing lessons. In the first place, you could only climb the volcano when it was a quiet day. The volcano was still active, and on some days, it was much more active than others. There was a company with guides who would take a group up the mountain. They were extremely safety conscious and they explained at the very first that not everyone would be able to make it to the top. It was a very steep and difficult climb. We would wear protective suits, which would help protect us from the snow and freezing temperatures going up, and the suits would also be some protection when the volcano did some "spitting." Unfortunately, if the volcano erupted, then nothing could really protect us, which was the reason for only climbing on very quiet days.

Also, there were special skills that needed to be learned to climb the ice. They covered the instructions over and over in the classroom and then went over them again as we began climbing. We were each given snowshoes and an ice pick. They explained that the mountain had fissures (or cracks) in it because of the volcano. The ice and snow would cover the openings and if you did not know exactly where they were, it was very easy to step in one and fall through the snow. The instructions were that we had to follow exactly in the steps of the lead guide. Over and over they told us not to step anywhere except exactly in the center of the footprint of the guide.

We were also instructed on how to use the ice pick. You would swing and put the pick in the area in front of you on the high side of the mountain. Then you would pick up your back foot and place it exactly in the footprint of the person immediately in front of you. Then you would swing and plant the pick again and move your other foot forward. That way you were always supported with the pick and one foot firmly in a secure footprint.

There was a lead guide and then several other guides that would go up with us. We were instructed exactly how close to remain to each other. If too much distance occurred between two climbers, one of the guides would signal for you to stop, and they would take you back down the mountain. If they determined that you were getting winded or having problems with the altitude, one of the guides would signal for you to stop, and they would take you back down the mountain. If you fell or slipped in any way, one of the guides would signal for you to stop, and they would take you back down the mountain. If you were not using your pick correctly or stepping in the exact center of the footprint in front of you . . . one of the guides would signal for you to stop, and they would take you back down the mountain. We were beginning to get the picture. They were very serious about not taking any chances.

We began the long climb. It would take several hours to get up there, and it would not be easy. There were about fifteen guests who were climbing and about eight or nine guides. We zigzagged up the mountain and within a short time, several guests were escorted back down the mountain by a guide because they were not following the instructions correctly. Either they were not able to keep the pace with the rest of the group, or they were not using the ice pick correctly, or not stepping directly in the center of the footprint of the person in front of them. You could tell the disappointment as each one was taken out of the group because it meant that they would not make it to the top and be able to see the volcano.

I learned a lesson from that process and knew that I wanted to try even harder to make it to the goal. I realized that in life we are trying to be successful and make it to the top or to a goal, but it is important to know what it takes to get there. It is helpful to have a guide to lead you so that you don't step wrong or lose your footing. And it is particularly helpful to follow the footsteps of those who have gone ahead.

We had almost made it to the top and over half of the group had been sent back down for various reasons, but the four of us were still moving upward, and I think we were pretty pleased with ourselves that we were still part of this adventurous group. But then all of a sudden, Holly stepped wrong and fell and started sliding down the mountain. She was able to flip over and catch herself with her ice pick so that she did not slide any farther. It was frightening for a moment, but as she stood back up, we knew she was OK. She said she was fine, and that she would be able to make her way back up to where we were, but the lead guide said no. It would be too dangerous, and so he motioned for one of the guides to go down to her and escort her on down the mountain. She tried to argue with him and begged that he let her keep going, but he was firm in his decision. The last we saw; the guide and Holly were headed down the mountain.

We summited not long after that and it was amazing. Not only was the view of the mountains and the world around us incredibly beautiful, but the sight of this huge black and red bubbling pit of a volcano set in the top of this icy mountain was one of the most astounding sights I have ever seen. They told us we could stop and rest on the edge of the crest, and after several hours of climbing we could take time to enjoy our picnic lunch that had been packed in our backpacks.

Jan, Carol, and I sat there and soaked in the magnificent view as we ate, but our hearts ached because the experience was not complete without our friend Holly by our side. I realized that adventure and the enjoyment of experiencing new things is not just the thrill of where you go and what you have an opportunity to see, but it also includes with whom you share that experience that matters. The three of us certainly were thrilled to make it to the top, but for the experience to truly be complete we needed our group to be complete.

Our one consolation was that we knew how much Holly would enjoy the hot tub and spa back at the resort where we were staying. We knew that was where we would find her when we got back. We also were pretty confident that even if Holly had not had the opportunity to finish this adventure, knowing her and how much she enjoyed life and looked for new opportunities, she probably would have some amazing stories to tell us about her adventures of everything that she had done after leaving us.

Life is full of adventures and opportunities. God is in it all and if we open our eyes, we can see God moving all around us demonstrating glory. What a blessing it is to look for the lessons in everything that we do and most of all what a blessing it is to have friends and family with whom we can share those amazing experiences!

Reflection Question:

What adventures does God have for you?

From Killing Fields to New Life

HAVE YOU EVER NOTICED how God will take the messiest, most painful times of our lives and reshape those experiences so that something good and beautiful is fashioned out of them? Actually, I have seen it happen numerous times—the mother who loses a child to a drunk driver and starts an organization such as MADD that lowers the culture's acceptance of driving while intoxicated and thus reduces the number of accidents. Or what about the women who take the stand against their abusers so that it lowers the likelihood of sexual abuse for women in the future. Or any number of situations which were horrible in the fact that they happened in the first place, but because people have the courage to face what they have gone through, they are able to make this world a better place.

Sometimes going back and facing that horrible situation can be very frightening. Our preference would be just to forget about it and never have to deal with it again. Yet sometimes God uses the most tragic things in life to ultimately generate the most glorious. As from the darkness of the cross comes the glory of the empty tomb and Jesus' resurrection. With God's power amazing things can happen.

I am especially inspired by a friend of mine named Chiv In. I feel blessed to have witnessed his transformation from horrendous conditions to become a blessing to so many lives. I had the pleasure of meeting him in 2009 when I moved back to the United States and became an associate pastor at First Church Carrollton. Chiv was a member of the church.

But allow me to back up and tell you about Chiv. He was born and raised in Cambodia. His childhood was good until the mid 1970s when the Cambodian revolutionary Pol Pot and the Khmer Rouge took control of the country. Under Pol Pot's regime, execution and famine killed about three million people. Families were split up. Many of the elite were executed, while most of the society was sent to the fields to work endless hours with very little food. A large number simply died of starvation, disease, and overwork.

Chiv was separated from his family and experienced incredible difficulties yet continued to survive. There were times that groups of about
a dozen would be taken out at nighttime by the Khmer Rouge, and they
would point-blank execute most of them. Yet they would let one or two
live so that they would go back and tell others what was happening. It was
a way of keeping fear stirred up among those who were being forced to
work. Three times Chiv was taken out with those random groups at nighttime. They never knew who would live and who would die. Yet it seemed
like God's hand of protection was on Chiv even though at that time he did
not know about God.

As a teenager, Chiv barely escaped the killing fields of Cambodia and
was able to cross over to Thailand and then immigrate to America in 1978.
Unfortunately, his family was not able to get out of the country.

Chiv did not know anything about Jesus, but his first introduction to
Christians was in the refugee camps watching the Christian aid workers
who lovingly fed and cared for those who were in need. He had not seen
such compassion shown from others prior to this.

Later in Texas he would meet Emara, a beautiful young lady who had
also escaped from Cambodia. Emara had accepted Jesus as her Lord and
Savior and she made it clear to Chiv that if he wanted a life with her, he
needed to become a Christian.

Fast forward to about 2008, when Chiv and Emara were a part of First
Church Carrollton. The church had a strong missions ministry and was encouraging all members to take part in some type of mission trip. Chiv heard
about a medical mission trip to Guatemala and decided that he wanted to
help with that particular ministry. He went by the church office to visit with
the pastor in charge of missions, Jeff Dietz, to sign up for the trip. Unfortunately, because of travel complications the Guatemala trip had just been
cancelled. Jeff just casually asked Chiv where he was from. Chiv answered
that he was from Cambodia. Jeff, who is younger and was not aware of the
history of Cambodia, nonchalantly commented, "Well, how about if we go
there?" Chiv just shook his head and politely said, "No."

Jeff would see Chiv around church and continued to ask him about
maybe exploring the idea of a mission trip to Cambodia. By about the third
time Chiv began thinking that maybe God wanted him to go back to his
home country, even though that was an incredibly frightening thought. As
Jeff and Chiv talked more about the possibility, Chiv explained the history
and about the killing fields. He also explained that he barely got out alive
thirty years ago. Yet after much prayer, Chiv agreed to go back to Cambodia and it was decided they would take a small investigative team to see if
there was a way to do some ministry over there. They were aware that 98

percent of Cambodia's population had not been exposed to the gospel of Jesus Christ, and so they prayed that doors would open for them to share the good news. As they were making plans for the trip, Jeff asked Emara if she would like to go with them. Her comment was that she would wait to see if her husband came back alive before she decided whether she would return to her home country.

The time came for Chiv, Jeff, and Mark Wyatt to go to Cambodia to check things out. Chiv still had some contacts in the capital city, and so they decided to go there. Some of Chiv's relatives showed up in Phnom Penh while they were there. He had not seen any of them for thirty years. Chiv's sister, Chantha, was among those who had traveled to Phnom Penh in hopes of seeing him. When she finally saw him, knowing that he now lived in America, she asked him what good thing he had for her. His response was that he brought her the best gift ever—Jesus Christ! He was able to tell her, and the others, about Jesus and they ended up baptizing her and her family. She begged Chiv to come back again to Cambodia and to come to her village and share this news with others.

A few months later another mission trip was planned to go to Cambodia, and this time there were sixteen from First Church Carrollton who went on the trip to share about Jesus. It was a difficult trip to go on the primitive roads several hours from Battambang to his sister's village of O-Khmom. But when the bus finally pulled up, they found that the whole village of a couple hundred people was there to greet them. They were so excited that these visitors had come to see them, and they had a tent set up so that they could hear what Chiv had to share with them.

Chiv had brought a little generator, a projector, and a copy of the *Jesus* film to show them in order to tell the story. Unfortunately, the generator stopped in the middle of the movie. So Chiv stood up and spoke in Khmer to the people and told them all about Jesus and his love and how he sacrificed himself on the cross and then three days later was raised from the dead.

At one point while Chiv was talking to the crowd about accepting Jesus as their Savior, a lot of the folks raised their hands. Chiv signaled for them to put their hands back down. Then he turned to the Americans and in English told them that he was not sure that the Cambodians understood him. He turned back around to the crowd and talked for a little while longer explaining to them what it meant to accept Jesus Christ as their Savior. He then said if there was anyone who was interested in making Jesus their Lord and being baptized that they should go over and stand on the side. In that moment, one hundred thirty-nine people stood up and moved to the side in order to get in line to be baptized and accept Jesus as the Lord of their life.

For the next several hours they were baptizing new believers and praying over this village that had so powerfully been impacted.

Chiv knew that he could not leave these new believers without someone to teach them and guide them as they grew in the faith. He ended up staying longer to set up key leaders in the church and to train them in how to care for the flock. Even after he returned to Texas, he would have regular phone calls with the leadership/pastoral team so that they were constantly learning. Everything that they were taught, they would then go out to each of the huts in the village and share the gospel message with the rest of the new Christians.

That was just the beginning! I had the privilege of going with Chiv and Emara on the next mission trip the following year. We shared more about Jesus, and we worked to put in a water well for the village. Also, by that time the word had spread, and even more people wanted to know about Christ. There was a village about two hours away through the jungle who had heard that something special was going on in O-Khmom, so they had walked over to hear the good news. The new Christians at O-Khmom shared what they had learned with the neighboring village of Kun Domrey. When we arrived, we wanted to go over to this new village and meet the believers. Unfortunately, the roads were not in good enough condition to travel there by car, so we jumped on the back of a few motorcycles and our Cambodian friends drove us through the jungle to reach Kun Domrey. It was such a blessing to meet and worship with these new fellow believers. We also had the opportunity to baptize even more of those who were coming to know the Lord.

Many in the villages gave their hearts to Jesus. One of those in Kun Domrey was a former Buddhist monk. He was so incredibly touched when he heard the story of Jesus Christ's sacrificial death and the power of his resurrection, that he felt he had to give his life to Christ and to share that glorious message with others. Though his Buddhist family has rejected him for his new belief, he had stayed strong in the faith and recognized the incredible difference that knowing Jesus had made in his life.

As the groups of Christians in the villages grew, they became too large to meet in homes and so Chiv coordinated with both his church in Texas, as well as the new congregations in the villages, to build church buildings. These churches have been a blessing to the congregations and the villages.

Since that first trip in 2008, God has moved in Chiv's life in so many powerful ways. He has studied and become a local pastor in the United Methodist Church, and his ministry is spread across multiple congregations. He is the senior pastor for the Cambodian Fellowship United Methodist Church in the Dallas area, an associate pastor of the First United Methodist

Church in Carrollton and is the head of Heart for Cambodia.[1] Chiv and Emara have made numerous trips back and forth to Cambodia to minister to the Christians there and to plant even more churches. Presently, there are eight established churches, and since he first went back, there have been more than six hundred who have accepted Jesus Christ as their Savior and been baptized into the faith.

Where I have seen God is in Chiv and his faith and loving spirit. He is an incredibly humble man and is a very dear friend. He has such a good heart and gives his all to ministering to those here in Texas. And one of the most fascinating things to watch is when he returns to Cambodia and projects a powerful personality because he is determined to share God's message with everyone he possibly can. Those of us who have had the privilege to travel with him have been in awe of how he takes control of the situation and seems to know exactly what to do. He is treated with great respect in his home country, and it is obvious that those who are there can tell that there is some sort of power around him. I guess it is almost as if they can see the power of God flowing from him, and it is this glow of joy that makes others want to know about this amazing Jesus Christ that Chiv calls his Lord.

It was a frightening thing for Chiv to go back to Cambodia in the first place. But he trusted God, and it has been astonishing to watch how God has used his faithfulness to open up so many ministries and touch so many lives. Praise God!

Reflection Question:

What is God challenging you to do?

---

1. More information about Pastor Chiv In and Heart for Cambodia may be found at heartforcambodia.org. It is a great opportunity to get involved and make a difference in sharing the good news of Jesus Christ and spread the gospel of love.

Baptizing in India

I FIRST MET LUKE and Kasthuri Raju one Sunday morning after I preached at First Church in Carrollton, Texas. They had been driving past on their way to another church and all of a sudden Kas suggested that they stop and attend First Church instead. My sermon that day was "How Big Is Your God?" and one of the stories I shared was about George Müller and his incredible prayer life and how he built orphanages in England by depending totally on God's provision.

I visited with Luke and Kas after the service when they came up to me in tears to tell how God had led them to that particular service and that was the message they needed to hear. Luke was leaving the next day to go back to India to continue work on building an orphanage. They shared briefly about their work. It is an incredible testimony of all that God has done to call them into this ministry, show them the exact land to build on, and provide them the necessary provisions. They were already well on their way in the ministry that God had called them to do, but they felt an extra blessing to have heard a message that seemed to be a special word of encouragement to continue in the way the Lord was leading.

That was the beginning of a special friendship. Luke and Kas ended up joining the church and we've had lots of opportunities to serve the Lord together. One of those opportunities was when Luke asked me if I would travel to India to see the building of the orphanage. He also invited me to preach and meet the pastors and the people of that area. Though I had traveled a lot and been to many countries on mission trips, I wasn't sure about going to India. I prayed about it and felt like God was guiding my steps to go and to help in any way that I might be able. I invited my daughter, LeeRand, to go with us. I knew it would be an opportunity to see God in action in a culture that was totally different than our own.

In February of 2011, Luke, LeeRand, and I headed to India. Luke was the perfect host in showing us the country where he had grown up. He and

Kas had moved to the United States over thirty years before, but God had kept their home country in their hearts, and so they were willing to go back to India to share God's love. They had supported ministers and the building of churches for years, but now God was telling them to build My Father's House Orphanage for the precious children who needed to be cared for and to feel God's love.[1]

While we were there, Luke introduced us to a number of different Christian ministers, and we had a chance to visit and encourage each other in the Lord. One of Luke's friends is Rev. Dr. A. Jawahar Samuel, who is known internationally for his prayer and healing ministry. God has been working in mighty ways through him in bringing people to the Lord. We had a chance to visit, and I was touched by the amazing miracles of healing God was doing through him. Dr. Samuel was going to northern India one of the Sundays, and I was given the privilege to preach for two morning services and an evening service in his stead at his church in Coimbatore. It is a huge building that holds 2,500 to 3,000 people for each service. I was speaking through an interpreter, but even with that many people crowded into one place it was perfectly silent as they hungrily listened for God's Word. There seemed to be a deep faith and passion for the Lord among those Christians who were worshiping and praying in this predominantly Hindu country.

That faith was demonstrated even more when we arrived at the site of My Father's House Orphanage near Kannavaram. Luke had arranged for a three-day revival to be held where the orphanage was being built. For years, Luke and Kas had supported forty-five ministers who preached in all of the villages in that area. Those ministers and their churches had traveled for hours on busses to come to the revival. There were several hundred people gathered. They slept on the ground for a couple of nights so that they could be together to worship the Lord. And every morning at 4:00 a.m. they would all get up to pray for a few hours before starting their day of worship and praise. The most important thing for these precious people was to know the Lord and to worship him. They were not worried about a comfortable, warm place to sleep, and I seem to remember that the only food was in the evening after they had fasted all day. What they were hungry for was Jesus Christ as their Savior.

When I think about the question of where I saw God—the Lord was all around! I was constantly struck by the humble faith of these people. They were willing to give up everything to follow Jesus as their Lord and Savior.

1. My Father's House Orphanage in Nellore, Andra Pradesh, South India, is supported by Faith Hope and Charity Ministries, a nonprofit Christian ministry based in Dallas, Texas. Contact through Luke Raju and faithhopeandcharityministries.org.

One of the greatest privileges was to baptize nineteen of them who had come from the different churches and chosen to be baptized during this revival. For many, it meant that they would be ostracized by their families. They were born into the Hindu faith and yet had come to know Jesus Christ. They were making the decision to begin life afresh with the Lord, even if it meant they were walking away from family and friends and all of their belongings. I met a beautiful young girl who was probably about fifteen years old and her faith glowed as she talked through an interpreter to tell me her story and her excitement to follow Jesus even though her father threatened to kill her because of the disgrace he thought this brought to their Hindu family. After she was baptized, she knew that she could never return to her home, yet she was ready to make that commitment and follow the Lord Jesus.

When it came time to baptize, we were not going to do it there on the stage that had been built for the revival. This was a life-changing moment for those who were being baptized, and they wanted more than just to be sprinkled; they wanted to go all the way under the water and come out washed clean and born new. It meant loading up in various vehicles and heading toward the river. One of the guys on a motorcycle gave me a ride as we led the caravan to the hill above the river. There we got off and walked a distance farther to come to the river's edge while following water buffalo also headed to the river. We reached an area that had a little clearing on the shore where we could wade through the mud to get out to deeper water. I stood in the water with a few other pastors as those on the shore prepared the nineteen for their baptism. One by one they came into the water.

When the first man came into the water, I asked his name so that I could call it out as he was being baptized. I expected him to just tell me his name. That is when Luke informed me that it was my responsibility to rename him. He had a Hindu name, but I should select a name from the Bible and from now on that would be his Christian name. He would never use his Hindu name again. It truly was a sign of beginning a whole new life. The first one I named was Matthew. To be honest, it felt like an awesome privilege and responsibility to be baptizing and naming each of these individuals. But who was I to be able to have this incredible authority of selecting a name that would forever be who they were known as? I was overwhelmed with emotion not only to have the privilege to baptize them, but also to rename them.

When I baptized the young girl, who had given up her family and all that she had in order to follow the Lord, I thought of the name Hannah. I remembered in the Bible how Hannah had been faithful to the Lord even

when it was a costly commitment.[2] I knew this young girl's decision to follow the Lord was also a costly commitment and I knew that God would be
with her and bless her.

Since I had not known about the naming requirement prior to my
beginning the baptisms, it is not as if I had a long list of names that I had
already thought about and prayed over. Instead, it meant that as each individual stepped into the water, I started praying fast, "Lord, give me the
name for this one." I wanted to make sure that the names that I bestowed on
each convert represented role models that they could live up to. It was easy
to come up with lots of men's names, but at some point, I was struggling to
come up with some women's names. I wanted each one to have their own
personal one that fit them. (Even though Rahab and Jezebel are names of
women in the Bible, I certainly did not want to use those.) God was gracious
in providing names for each of them.

It was such a poignant experience to stand in that river water and to
baptize those new believers whose greatest desire was to follow the Lord.
Afterward, as we made our way out of the water and began walking back
up the riverbank, one of the older men commented that I was a very brave
woman. I looked at him quizzically and said, "Are you kidding, it is the
greatest privilege ever to baptize someone." He then told me that I could be
arrested for converting a Hindu to a Christian. I had not been aware of that
before I baptized these wonderful people, but I also knew in my heart that
it would not have changed anything. I think it would be more frightening
to know that I had a chance to help someone grow in his or her faith and
did not obey the Lord. It was just another reminder of how blessed and easy
it is for those of us in Christian countries to have the freedom to worship
and follow Jesus, and how unaware we are of the dangers and the amount
of faith needed for our Christian sisters and brothers in other countries.
Yet somehow, I envy them . . . I have a feeling their faith in the Lord is so
much stronger than mine because of the sacrifices they have made to truly
follow Jesus Christ as their Lord and Savior. Gracious God, protect them
and strengthen them!

Reflection Question:

How might God be asking you to sacrifice in order to follow him?

---

2. 1 Samuel 1.

Divine Encounter 41

New Eyes to See God

WHEN MY DAUGHTER, LeeRand, and I traveled to India with Luke Raju in 2011, we were primarily going there to support the orphanage that God had called Luke and his wife, Kas, to build. Yet part of their ministry throughout the years had also been to support various ministers in the area. Luke and Kas worked hard in the United States to make money in order to support all of the churches and ministries.

It was such a privilege for me to meet with the various pastors and hear about their ministries. They shared the good things that were happening as well as their struggles in a country that can often be harsh to Christians.

One of the pastors was a man named Pastor Israel. It was obvious from the way the other pastors treated him that he was well respected. He had an incredibly humble spirit and a deep joy. I couldn't wait to hear how he had come to know the Lord and be called into ministry.

He shared with me that he had been blind from a very early age. In India children often must fend for themselves, especially if they have a disability. He was left to wander the streets. Though he survived, it definitely was not easy, and he hated his life.

His name was not Israel at that time, but instead he had a Hindu name. When he was in his early twenties, he decided to end his life. It was not worth living. He could not see but he had a keen sense of hearing, and he knew that a train came by every day. He decided that the next day he would walk near the train tracks and when he heard the locomotive coming, he would step in front of it and end his life.

He went down there the next day expecting to commit suicide. He waited, listening closely for the train in the distance. He waited and waited, but the train never came. Instead, as he was sitting with his ears perked up, what he heard was not the train but a street preacher in the distance reading from the Bible and talking about this man named Jesus. The preacher told how Jesus could give sight to the blind and help the deaf to hear and the lame to walk and heal those with leprosy. He had never heard of this Jesus before.

That night he could not stop thinking about the strange fact that the train never came, but instead that he had heard about this Jesus. He decided that he would try to pray to Jesus. He had been raised as a Hindu, and all of his life he had prayed to the millions of Hindu gods and never had one answered him or helped him in any way. What did he have to lose to pray to one more god? So, he prayed to Jesus. He said that he didn't know who Jesus was or if he was a real god, but if Jesus would heal him and give him his eyesight, then for the rest of his life he would serve him.

The next morning when he awoke his eyesight was not great, but he could see more than he had been able to see in years. And over the next few weeks, his eyesight got better and better until it was totally restored. It had been a miraculous healing where his total sight had been given back to him in a very short time starting with his prayer to Jesus. True to his vow, he became a follower of Jesus Christ and was baptized with the name of Israel. He then became a pastor. When I met Pastor Israel, he had been a pastor for thirty-seven years. He had started sixty-five churches. He was also the mentor and guide to all of the other pastors. Through his witness, Pastor Israel had led an incredible number of people to the Lord. Not only those who had known him when he was blind and had seen what God had done in his life, but also those to whom he shared the wonderful good news about Jesus Christ. He was an incredibly godly man who when you looked him in his eyes, you knew he had seen God in an amazing way and that he walked each day in faith.

Reflection Question:

Where have you seen God's answer to prayer?

Divine Encounter 42

God Knows the Depth

FROM THE FIRST TIME that I met Luke Raju, I realized what a man of faith he was in building My Father's House Orphanage in India. He and his wife, Kas, spent lots of hours in prayer trying to listen to God directing their lives and particularly giving them instructions on where and how the orphanage should be built. They have some amazing testimonies of how the Lord showed them exactly what property was the right one to purchase and then putting the right people in place to handle different things. God's fingerprints are all over this home for precious children.

One of my favorite stories is about the water well. At the time that my daughter and I had gone to India to help support the orphanage, there had been a well. I remember standing by it and watching workmen use the water as they made their own bricks for the construction of the orphanage. A little later that well dried up, and it became necessary to dig another well.

Four years before, when the original well was put in place, Luke had been in Texas at the time and the man who was overseeing the building, Jarod, had coordinated the placement of the well with a company from Chennai. Luke had learned afterward that a Hindu priest had come on the property to locate where the well would be and to pray to Hindu gods before any work was done. A new well needed to be placed, and there was not a Christian company that could do the work. The same company would have to be used again, but Luke made sure that he was on the property when the Hindu priest and workers arrived. This orphanage was being built at the direction of the Lord God Almighty, and this property was dedicated to Jesus Christ. So, Luke wanted to make sure everything that was done on this property would glorify God.

When the Hindu priest and workmen showed up with their big drilling trucks and equipment, Luke met them at the gate of the property. He said the workmen and the equipment they needed were welcome on the property. But he explained that since it was a Christian property the Hindu priest would not be allowed to come on the land. Of course, they were all very upset and refused to do the work unless the priest came onto the property and participated with his religious rituals. Luke stood firm that this orphanage and all that surrounded it belonged to Jesus Christ, and no other gods would be worshipped or acknowledged on this land. The workmen called back to their boss in Chennai to explain the situation and to request permission just to return without doing the work. However, the boss was aware he had just sent all these men and equipment a considerable distance, and if they returned without doing the work then he had just lost a day's work for all of them and would not get any money for the job. So, the boss instructed them to do as Luke said and to do the work without the participation of the Hindu priest. The boss was not happy about it, but at least this way he would get paid for the job.

Luke allowed the others on to the property. But part of the issue with the Hindu priest is he was the one who would determine where the well should be placed. He would take a coconut and place incense on top of it and then would hold it upright in the palm of his hand as he walked around the property. He would sing a Hindu ritual song as he walked around. Supposedly the gods would tell him where to dig the well by knocking over the coconut in the place where the water was located. Since Luke would not allow the Hindu priest to come on the property, the workmen were concerned about where to locate the well. Luke prayed about it and took them to the location where he felt God was telling him the well should be placed.

When the workmen saw the place, they argued with Luke and said they were sure that place did not have water near the surface. This company had dug a well on a different property three miles away only two days before, and they had to go all the way to 225 feet. They were pretty sure this place which Luke had picked would be about the same. But Luke informed them that this is where God had told him the well should be, and they would hit water by eighty feet and the well would not need to be deeper than one hundred feet.

Once again, the men argued and refused to work. They did not like the location Luke had shown them, and they were scared to work without the blessing of the Hindu priest. Luke tried to reassure them his God, Jesus Christ, was big enough to handle all of this. But they decided they were not willing to do the work. They called their boss in Chennai again and tried to get out of doing the work. Once again, their boss was not happy, he made Luke promise to take responsibility in case someone got hurt since they did not have the prayers of protection from the Hindu priest. Luke assured him the Lord God Almighty is big enough to handle all things. The boss was determined he did not want it to be a wasted trip, so he instructed the workmen to dig at the location that Luke had instructed.

Luke, Jarod, and a few other Christians gathered around the location and began praying God would do a mighty demonstration of power. A well is dug by forcing twenty-foot poles into the ground until the water table is reached. The first pole was placed, and then the second, and then the third, which meant the depth was now sixty feet deep. As the fourth pole was being pushed into the ground, at about a depth of seventy-five feet, wet sands began to come out of the hole. As the pipe went just a little deeper, water began to shoot upward from the ground. Living water was pouring out of the pipe. They had hit a wonderful well of water proving that God's direction was right.

It was an incredible witness to the Hindu workmen that day and was also an encouragement to all of the Christians. Jarod had been frightened that if it did not work, he would not be able to show his face around town, and everyone would laugh at him. Yet God came through in a mighty way. And the well that was placed that day still flows and continues to be the source of water for My Father's House Orphanage.

Reflection Question:

Where is God calling you to take a stand of faith?

Divine Encounter 43

God Speaks All Languages

YOU REALIZE, OF COURSE, that for most of us, we shrink God down to our size, and we imagine that the Lord looks and thinks like us. I mean after all, certainly the Lord God Almighty speaks with a Texas accent! Or maybe that is just what I expect.

I do not know why I had not really thought about it much before, but I was caught off guard one day when I was in chapel at seminary. We happened to have a choir from Russia come to the Southern Methodist University campus, and they had just finished a beautiful performance. Most of the songs they sang were in their native Russian language, but I think there were a few of the songs in English. The service had continued with a sermon and then at some point we had all bowed our heads to pray together the Lord's Prayer.

The Lord's Prayer is a prayer that our congregations are used to saying together with a certain rhythm. Yet this time there was something that was not exactly right about it. It was as if some people in the chapel that day were not saying it in the usual cadence, so it felt very awkward. I could not determine who was off, but obviously someone was not saying it correctly, and it was really aggravating. Where I should have been focused on my prayer to the Lord God Almighty, I was much more distracted by trying to figure out who in this room was messing up our prayer!

We got to the last few lines of the prayer . . . "and lead us not into temptation, but deliver us from evil, for thine is the kingdom and the power and the glory for ever and ever. Amen." And then I heard it! The words continued from a whole group of people in the chapel that day, only they were not speaking in English (or Texan). They were saying the last few lines of the same prayer, but because it was in a different language, it sounded different, and it ended a little later than what we had just spoken. And I stood there in shock as I thought to myself, "Oh my goodness, they are saying the Lord's Prayer, but they are saying it in Russian instead of

English! God understands Russian too!" I was so incredibly shocked by the realization. I know it sounds silly, but I had never really thought about it before, and it was such an amazing observation and appreciation for how big our God really is.

Language is so important. When we are trying to communicate something to someone else, it helps to be able to speak the same language. God certainly created and understands all languages, but sometimes we as the Lord's children may have difficulty in trying to communicate with those who do not speak our language. Yet God is big enough to handle all things.

I had the privilege of working with Dr. Richard Dunagin, who was the senior pastor of First Church in Carrollton, Texas. I remembered his testimony about when he had been invited in 2007 to come preach for a week at the Methodist Church in Korea. The theme for the week was focused on prayer. Richard is an excellent preacher, but he felt very inadequate to be preaching to the Koreans about prayer. After all, the Korean Church arises en masse every morning, 365 days a year, and assembles itself at the church building to pray. As Richard says, "We talk about prayer; the Koreans actually do it."

Richard wanted to try to support the ministry and further the witness of God any way that he possibly could, so he traveled to Korea. When he arrived, the pastor informed him that he would be acting as his translator during the services. Pastor Jeong spoke English fairly well, yet not everything was clear to him in conversation and so sometimes he needed clarification. Thus, he asked if Richard could give him a manuscript of the sermon each day in advance so he could read over it and make sure he understood all of the concepts and could translate everything correctly from English to Korean.

One afternoon Richard finished writing his message for the day, and he went to Pastor Jeong's office to print out the manuscript. Unfortunately, his computer locked up and Richard could not get anything to print. Both Richard and Pastor Jeong were concerned and nervous about that evening's service. They did not want people to miss out on God's message just because of a technological glitch and not being able to clearly translate the concepts to Korean. Richard was really disturbed that he had not come to Korea with completed manuscripts in hand.

The church was full that evening, and all they could do was to go out and try their very best. When Richard got up to speak, Pastor Jeong was standing right beside him ready to translate, just as they had done the previous few days. Richard started talking, and as he had done in the days before, Pastor Jeong spoke in Korean after each sentence that Richard spoke. Richard noticed as he got into the message, that Pastor Jeong matched his intensity and emotion every step of the way. And when Richard finished, Pastor Jeong continued speaking, only now it was with even greater emotion. Richard noticed there were tears in Pastor Jeong's eyes, and the people were obviously profoundly moved as he spoke. The whole church then sang and prayed fervently afterward until finally the service was done.

After most people had left the service, Richard asked Pastor Jeong what was going on because it was obvious something powerful and unique had transpired that evening. It was evident the Holy Spirit's presence was strongly in their midst.

Pastor Jeong told Richard how very worried he had been before the service when the printer would not work. He had planned for these services and really wanted God to move in them. He went on to explain that when they got up to speak God did an amazing thing. Pastor Jeong said, "I know you do not speak Korean. And my English is not all that good. But Richard, when you opened your mouth to preach tonight, what I heard coming out of your mouth was Korean, not English. All I had to do was repeat it to the congregation, easy as can be. After you finished preaching, I told the people what had happened. That's why there was such a hush that fell over the whole body. And then, naturally, we burst out in praise to our great God. A mighty miracle took place right here in our service tonight! Praise be to God!"

Why do we limit God? God is so much bigger than we can ever imagine! And God is the God of all languages.

Reflection Question:

How big is your God?

Divine Encounter 44

Walk a Mile in My Shoes

NOTHING CAN BE MORE exciting for me than an adventure combined with a physical challenge, and a spiritual perspective. Certainly, the Camino de Santiago offers all three and so much more. *Camino de Santiago* translates to the "Way of Saint James." It refers to the pilgrimage one takes to arrive at the cathedral in the city of Santiago de Compostela in Galicia in northwest Spain. That is the location of the remains of James the Apostle's body. The first recorded pilgrimage to this location was in the ninth century. It has continued as a popular Christian pilgrimage since the Middle Ages until today. There are several different routes to get there depending on where you start. Many of those routes begin in other countries. Most often the journey is walked on foot with a backpack, but there are also those who ride bicycles, and a few who ride horses to make the pilgrimage. Where a pilgrim begins determines how many days, weeks, and months someone might be in route.

I had heard of the Camino de Santiago before, but particularly became interested in it when I saw the movie *The Way*, with Martin Sheen and Emilio Estevez. I decided I really wanted to have the opportunity to walk this ancient way that has been traveled for centuries. Pilgrims from all over the world travel this path. I would have loved to have started in St. Jean, France, and to spend about five or six weeks making my way across the varied countryside of Spain, but I knew I was limited to ten to twelve days at the most. I visited with a couple of friends who had made the trek and decided I would start in Astorga and head to Santiago.

My trip to Spain for the walk on the Camino was part of a larger trip, which included England, Northern Ireland, and Ireland. It also included a variety of activities such as visiting old friends, preaching, and writing. Because I was doing other traveling and activities, I was limited in what equipment I could bring with me from Texas. I brought my large backpack and some of my hiking equipment, but my bags were already too full of other things, so I could not include my favorite hiking boots. I decided before

I even left America that if I did get the chance to walk the Camino that I would just have to purchase some new boots while in England.

During my time in England, when I was staying with good friends, I began gathering the things that I would need for walking the Camino. Dave and Anne Wright were going to take me shopping at an outdoor equipment store. When I mentioned that I needed new boots, they commented that it might be dangerous to walk that distance in new boots which had not been properly broken in. I had certainly recognized that fact when I had to make the tough decision to leave my favorite boots at home, but I knew it was a chance I would have to take. Anne suggested that I try on her good walking boots. Being typical English, they had done a lot of walking and only recently had slowed down from the usual weekly treks out to the countryside. Anne had a great-looking pair of leather walking boots, which were incredibly comfortable. I decided to take them with me one week when I went up to the northeastern coast of England where I was doing some writing and walking. I tried the boots for several days on some fairly long hikes and decided that they would be great for Spain. Anne laughed that she might not ever walk the Camino de Santiago, but at least she could say that her boots had. She was delighted for me to borrow them for the trip, and I was excited to have such comfortable footwear. I would enjoy using them and then would return her "Camino-experienced" boots back to her.

I took off to Spain and traveled to the city of Astorga to begin the long walk. I arrived by train around noon, and I was so excited to get there and start the lengthy pilgrim walk. I took off with my backpack, my walking sticks, and my comfortable boots. About three hours into the walk, I started to notice something dragging on my right heel. I figured I must have stepped on something, but when I lifted my boot what I discovered was that the sole of the right shoe was literally pulled away from the rest of the shoe. As I held it up, it was flapping like a gaping mouth opening and closing. I was horrified. It was just the first day, and my boot was falling apart! How in the world would I be able to walk through much more difficult territory for ten to twelve more days with this shoe?

There was nowhere to go and buy new boots. I knew I would just have to do the best I possibly could. I remembered that a good friend, Darren Middleton, had given me some really strong tape to take for the walk when I visited with his family in England. Darren is the Padre for the 29 Commando Regiment Royal Artillery and had just completed the thirteen-week Commando course for the British Army. He had mastered some unbelievably difficult physical challenges. He had encouraged me to use the tape on my feet in order to prevent blisters or the loss of toe nails. I had planned to use it to protect my feet, but it was obvious that I now needed to use it to tape my boot together. I had to prevent the heel from pulling away more and eventually causing the entire sole to detach itself. When I stopped and taped up the boot, I said a little prayer that it would hold and that God would provide a way for me to continue the walk.

A few hours later, I stopped for water and orange juice. While resting for a moment, I looked down to check my boot. The tape seemed to be holding, thank you, Lord! But when I looked at the left boot, I realized that the entire sole was pulling away from the outside of that shoe. Oh goodness! This was not good. I taped up the left shoe and then walked just a little farther to an albergue (a place for pilgrims to stay). Since this was my first day to walk, I had hoped to go farther, but knew I better stop for the evening.

In an albergue you are often in a room with lots of other pilgrims. The cost is only six to eight euros to rent a bed and have a place to shower and wash out your walking clothes. I had dinner with a group of pilgrims and got some sleep. Many pilgrims start their day's walk very early in the morning. I decided I might as well begin the walk in the dark. Before I had left the albergue, I put on my boots and taped them extremely well. With so much tape wrapped around them, I had hoped I would not need to take the boots off for any reason. I prayed the tape would hold the soles on. There was a full moon to show the path, and it was amazingly calm and quiet to be walking that morning. What a wonderful time to just walk and talk with God, about boots and everything else.

A couple of hours later as the sun was just starting to come up, I was passing through a small village and found a café/bar open for breakfast. I went in to get something to eat and while I was there, a woman from Germany, who I had met at dinner the night before, came in. Over breakfast we decided we would walk together for a while. Her name was Elke Weindel. She was tall and looked to be in great shape for such an adventure like this.

Elke had done portions of the Camino four other times before, but this time she would be able to finish the walk to Santiago. We had a great time visiting. Then somehow, I mentioned God, and when I did, she let me know very quickly that she did not believe in God. I said that was fine—whatever she chose to believe, but I definitely did believe in God and had seen the Lord move in my life in many ways. I was not going to try to force my beliefs on her, but I also knew that God is the strength and guide in my life.

Since Elke had walked parts of the Camino before and had really studied it, she was able to tell me a lot about the different symbols and stories. She excitedly talked about her past experiences as well as some of the fascinating locations ahead of us.

As we moved along the trail, I suddenly realized that even with all the tape on my boots, the ground was so rocky and rough that the soles of my boots were completely separated. They were literally held only by the tape. We stopped and Elke helped me re-tape them in hopes I could continue the walk. There was no place to get new boots, and no vehicles anywhere near to catch a ride. I would just have to keep walking.

Elke told me another piece of folklore from the Camino. She said there was a saying that "the Camino provides whatever you need!" So, she stated maybe the Camino would provide me a new pair of boots. I laughed and said I did not believe the Camino could do that, but I did believe in God. The Lord is the Lord God Almighty, the Creator of the entire universe, who certainly created the Camino, and I knew I could pray, and God's Holy Spirit would provide me with what I needed.

About twenty minutes later we passed a strange little shack along the path of the Camino near the abandoned village of Manjarin. It was obvious pilgrims (or "peregrinos" as they are called in Spanish) were welcomed here. In most of the café/bars along the route, you can buy water and refreshments. But when we went in the little shack, there was a large table with water, cookies, and refreshments for the pilgrims for free. The owner, a man from Argentina, explained it was all out there for us, whatever we needed. He was just trying to support and help the pilgrims in any way he could. He kept nodding to the refreshments and saying, "Whatever you need." I laughed and pointed to my shoes and said, I guess he didn't have any shoes for me. He looked at my boots and was shocked to see that they were falling apart and that they had been wrapped over and over with tape. We laughed about it for a little while and then all of a sudden, he got a surprised look on his face and said, "Wait a minute!"

He ran into a curtained area and in a little while came back holding a pair of great-looking new cream-colored Salomon hiking boots. (By the way, Salomon is a top brand in shoes and boots for running, hiking, and outdoor sports.) He said he did not know what size they were, but if they fit, I could have them. To be honest, they looked a little small and I hated to undo all the tape I had wrapped around my boots to try them on. What if they did not work? But I figured I might as well give them a shot. After all, what were the possibilities that a new pair of hiking boots could be found in a place like this out in the wilderness? There must be a reason they were here, and I figured they were an answer to prayer. Sure enough, the Salomon boots fit perfectly! I was surprised how comfortable they were. I could not have picked out better boots had I been in a store with a large inventory. I offered to pay him because I knew they were very expensive, but he said, "No, they are for you."

He asked what I was going to do with my old boots, and I told him I was going to throw them away. (If you are walking a long distance with a backpack, you really do not want anything in it which is not essential. My backpack was already too heavy, and I was not about to add additional weight. I was hoping Anne would understand when I did not bring back her dusty, crumbling boots.) He asked if he could have the old boots to put on his shelf in the shack so he could tell other pilgrims the story. I said he was more than welcome to them—tape and all. So, he snapped a picture of me beside my dilapidated footwear.

I was delighted to have a new pair of boots for walking the Camino, but even better, was seeing the expression on Elke's face. After that, Elke shared the story of the boots and how God had provided them with everyone we met. She was so thrilled with what she had just witnessed that she, and other pilgrims, kept asking me to share God-stories about where I had seen God. In fact, it became a regular part of each day on the Camino to have various people walk up and introduce me to someone new and ask me to tell one of the stories. Immediately prior to going to Spain, I had spent the week on the northern cliffs of England writing down many of the stories about some of the amazing things I had seen God doing in my life and the lives of those around me. So, I had plenty of examples fresh on my mind to testify to how God is personally involved in our lives . . . if we allow the Lord to guide us.

Six or seven days after I had been given the shoes, we happened to cross paths with a man we had not met before. As we were talking about where we had come from and the amazing sites and extraordinary experiences we had seen along the Camino, he started telling a story he had heard about a woman who was walking the Camino and her hiking boots started falling apart. He did not get very far into the story before those near me started pointing at me saying, "She is the one! Look at her boots!" By now they were pretty dusty and dirty from about a hundred miles of walking. But it was fun confirming the story about God providing new boots on the Camino. I have to smile every time I think about how that event opened up the opportunity for me to share lots of other God-stories with Elke and many of the other pilgrims walking the Camino.

By the way, Elke and I finished the journey to Santiago de Compostela on the tenth day after walking 272 km (170 miles) from Astorga. That evening we were able to attend the Pilgrims Mass at the cathedral with two other special friends we had met along the way: Carol O' Byrne from Ireland and Agustin Gonzalez from Spain. Later that night when we said our good-byes knowing we would all head off to our home countries, one of the questions asked was, "What will you carry home with you from the Camino?" How exciting to hear them all say that they would go home with more of a heart and desire to grow and experience God!

You never know where you will see God moving, even on a dusty trail in Spain. And you also never know how many lives will be touched when they realize God does exist and is very involved in even the little everyday things . . . like the shoes we wear.[1]

Reflection Question:

What will you trust God to provide?

1. Just a note to say that a year and a half after I had walked the Camino, I received a text from a friend who had returned to walk it again. She wanted to let me know that the story about the " shoes provided by God" was still being shared among the pilgrims.

Looking Ahead

Faith Pointing

GOD IS MOVING ALL around us, but we often seem oblivious to the miracles and glorious illustrations of divine power. We live in this amazing world and yet somehow, we seem to take so much of it for granted. There are times when I realize I am missing the glory of God right in front of me. When that happens, I start trying to become more attentive to the Lord's movements and blessings so that I do not stumble through the day totally unaware. It seems I may remember to keep my eyes open for a little while, but soon I have reverted back to my usual mode of being wrapped up in my own little world while ignoring all the amazing things the Lord is displaying around me.

It may help to have someone beside us who recognizes all the fabulous demonstrations of God's creativity and activity. They can point out those things that we so easily miss. It is like looking at life through a child's eyes and seeing all the wonder and magnificence there is in the world. When we were young, we were fascinated by nature and even the tiniest things would catch our imagination. It was fun to watch the ants as they followed each other in a line, or to fill your pockets with pretty rocks, or play with the roly-poly bugs, or look for the perfect walking stick which could also double as a sword or a baton. It seemed like we paid more attention to the world around us back then. Yet as we have grown older and gotten busier with life, unfortunately some of us have stopped "seeing" how special things are all around us. Thank goodness there are still those who recognize the splendor of God's creation and can gently remind us.

High Rise Day Habilitation is an outstanding ministry at the First United Methodist Church in Cedar Hill. It was started by Jeri Barnett and Jessica Pena because they recognized the need for day-to-day support, as well as a safe, nurturing environment for adults with developmental and intellectual challenges. Many of the young adults who participate in High Rise were students of Jeri's when she taught Special Education at Cedar Hill ISD. They are a wonderful, loving group and Jessica and Jeri are constantly teaching them new things and opening the door for incredible opportunities and experiences. Weekly they take excursions to different places such as the lake, petting zoo, theater, bowling alley, museum, swim park, and the list could go on and on. They do art work, make T-shirts, sing and dance, play with water balloons, and learn about life from lots of fun, creative activities.

One day after the parents and family members had picked up all of the students, Jeri, Jessica, and I were standing in the hall visiting. I was asking what great things they had been doing that day and what exciting excursions they had planned for the rest of the week. They said the group was planning on going to the Dallas Zoo that Friday and happened to mention they needed one more chaperone to go with them to the zoo. Friday is usually one of my critical days for working on the sermon, but I realized it would be such a blessing to be able to escort this precious group to the zoo. I quickly volunteered.

On Friday, we loaded up the van and headed toward the Dallas Zoo. It was a gorgeous day and there was lots of excitement about our upcoming adventure. There were sixteen of us walking around the zoo and enjoying the opportunity to see the various animals.

One of the attractions was a bird show in the amphitheater, so we ushered everyone in to get seats before the show began. After everyone else was seated and taken care of, I looked for a place to sit with our group. There was an open seat on a row next to Faith, one of the young girls from High Rise. I made my way down to sit next to her.

I knew some of the students better than others just from being around them for various activities and seeing them in the building. I had not had an opportunity to get to know Faith as well, but I had observed her interactions with others. She seemed to have such a sweet spirit and I would watch how she would get close to some of the other students and would gently touch them on the arm and then point out things to them. It seemed to be her way of communicating and making sure others recognized what was going on around them. I had been impressed with how aware and attentive she was of her surroundings and how sensitive and caring she was of others to make sure that they also were in tune with their environment and what was happening.

As soon as I sat down next to Faith she smiled and seemed to open up to include me into her world. I have never heard Faith speak, but she does an excellent job of making sure you know what she is experiencing. Her mother, Marti, later explained that when Faith was a baby, she would often have four to five petit mal seizures a day. When she was two years old the doctor had told her mother that Faith would never walk or talk. Yet her mother had felt God's hand on this adorable girl from the moment she was born. In fact, her name is Faith because her mother had heard God saying that was her name and that her life would be special. As Faith grew, she continued to suffer from epileptic seizures, occasionally she would have grand mal seizures. She was on seizure medication and her mother covered her in prayers daily.

When Faith was eight years old her mother was praying and heard God say that Faith was healed of the seizures. She talked with the doctor about it and asked if Faith could be taken off of the seizure medication. The doctor agreed to try it and they slowly weened her off the medication and sure enough she no longer had seizures. Now when they go for doctor appointments that same doctor is so amazed when Faith walks into the office and seems to be so very aware of everything going on. Though her speech is limited she seems to have a very deep understanding of all that is happening around her and she does an excellent job of communicating by touching and pointing.

At the zoo that day as I sat down by Faith, she scooted closer to me and began making sure that I did not miss a single mystery of God's creation right there in front of us. She would gently touch me on the arm or the leg to get my attention and then point toward whatever she wanted me to see. This process was repeated over and over and over: touch, point at the zoo employee with the safari costume, touch, point at the bird that flew up on stage, touch, point at a different bird that just came out. And every once in a while, between the touching and pointing, Faith would turn her head to make eye contact and would smile a beautiful smile and nod, and it was as if she was checking to make sure that I was understanding and recognizing all the impressive grandeur that was going on right before our eyes. It was apparently such a joy to her not only to watch all that was happening . . . but also to share the opportunity with someone else. She did not just want me to "see" the show; she wanted me to fully experience it in all of its glory. I felt incredibly blessed to be the one on the receiving end of this angelic revelation.

Later there were some pictures posted on the High Rise Facebook page showing some of the fun things that we had done at the zoo that day. There was one taken by Jessica from the end of the row looking at several of us as we were fascinated by all that was happening on stage. It showed Faith and me, with our heads leaned toward each other, as we were both looking at whatever the latest thing that she was pointing out. I was overwhelmed with thankfulness when I saw the picture. I realized I could have sat there and watched that bird show on my own and it would have been no big deal. I have had the incredible privilege of traveling extensively in my lifetime and seeing some astounding sites. I am afraid I would have

quickly dismissed this zoo experience as just another day had I not had
Faith by my side. It was her unquenchable joy and delight which made it
really special and a day I will never forget.

Maybe that is part of the blessing of having faith is that it opens our
eyes to what God is doing all around us. Before we learn to trust in the Lord,
we are just depending on ourselves. We think we know all there is to know
about life. And yet when we come to know the Lord, we start to recognize
the mystery and awe which is part of our relationship. We are constantly
amazed at all the divine things going on around us. And maybe that is when
we realize that God has sent his angels to be by our side and gently touch us
and point out the Lord's glory . . . as Faith did for me. I think those are the
times when we really start to see God.[1]

Reflection Question:

What is God's angel pointing out to you?

---

1. One more God-sighting, after this chapter was written, I sent it to Faith's mother
so she would know what would be shared. She texted back the following: "I just sat
down and read it twice and both times I cried. I know you don't know but Faith's di-
agnoses is called Angelman Syndrome. Thank you so much for seeing it as she does."

Divine Encounter 46

Epilogue: In Your Life . . .
Where Have You Seen God?

SO NOW THAT YOU have had an opportunity to hear some of the many stories about where I have seen God moving in my daily life, I want to ask you the same question—"Where have you seen God?" My hope is that as you have gone through this book and read the stories and the questions at the end of each divine encounter, it has inspired you to think and be more aware of what is going on around you. Believe me, there is nothing special about me that I have had all of these incredible God experiences. It is just that I have become more sensitive to the Lord as I spend more time with him.

It is no different than when you grow in a relationship with someone and you really get to know them. After a while, you know how they will handle things and what they like and what they would say or do in a particular situation. Certainly, I do not proclaim to know everything about God, but by reading the Bible and spending lots of time in prayer and trying to listen, I do believe I have gotten much better at hearing the Lord's voice. As I have said, it is not always an audible voice, though sometimes it has been, but I think more often it is an assurance of knowing God's will or feeling the Lord's guidance.

My recommendation, if you would like to experience God more, is just to open yourself up to the Lord. That means spending time with God and really focusing on seeing, hearing, and paying attention to what is going on around you and trying to look for God in all situations. It is a matter of taking time to shut out the noisy world and make sure that daily you have some time with just you and the Lord.

I also believe that the more obedient we are to the Lord and the more willing to step out in faith that it will also increase our experiences of God. In fact, sometimes I don't think God is revealed until we have taken that step of faith. It is similar to the priests carrying the arc of the covenant and

185

crossing the Jordan River in the book of Joshua.[1] Those priests, especially the ones in front, were probably wishing they could stand on the shore until a sign from God came and the water stopped flowing, but instead they had to take the first step in obedience to what God had told them to do. And the moment that they did, and their feet touched the water, is when the floodwaters stopped flowing and they were able to walk across on dry ground. God has a way of showing up big time if we will just be faithful and give the Lord the opportunity.

It is not just in the big events in our lives where we can see God. If we open our eyes, the Lord is active in even the small everyday things. We have the privilege of living in this amazing world where God is moving all around us. God is in the people we meet each day, the opportunities that are open to us, and the magnificent nature surrounding us. And yet, if you are like me, I get so caught up in the daily "stuff" that I miss the really great things that are going on right in front of me. It is as if we are sleepwalking through life and only halfway paying attention. I know that God is always with us and has many blessings for us. Too often we walk past and never even recognize the gifts which are ours.

In the last few years, it is as if God has been helping me to see life a little clearer; to realize there are some powerful events inviting me to join in with the fun things that God is constantly creating for us. Those events are easy to miss. But I am learning to ask myself that question "Where have I seen God?" and to train myself to share those blessings and document them. Both sharing and documenting are important.

From reading Scripture, I realize that God does not give someone a gift that is only for them. Everything we have is meant to be shared with others. That is why the Bible talks about the fact that we are blessed to be a blessing. So certainly, that applies to our "God sightings" and those precious moments when God touches us deeply. We are not supposed to wrap our arms around those moments and turn our backs on the world while proclaiming, "Mine, all mine." Instead, they are intended to be shared in order to bless other people's lives. I have noticed when we share those stories and experiences, then it helps us all to be more aware of what the Lord is doing in our lives.

So be sure to share your God experiences and those times where you have seen God. It will bless others, but it will also bless you to see how it touches their lives. There are plenty of places you can share your experiences—tell your family and your friends, communicate with the groups in your church and community, and certainly you are always welcome to share those

1. Josh 3:9–16.

stories with me. I love to hear how God is moving in other people's lives. You are welcome to go to drkevagreen.com or search https://www.facebook.com/ drkevagreen/ to post your story and read other people's stories.

When you document your story, it is an opportunity to share, and for you to keep a record of what the Lord is doing in your life. Sometimes we go through difficult times in our lives and one of the greatest gifts is to go back and read some of those journals or notes where we documented what the Lord has been personally doing for us. It is a source of encouragement and a reminder of God's involvement in our lives. Of course, it is wonderful to read the Bible and see how God touched other people's lives, but I know from personal experience that it can be an incredible blessing to sit and read my journals and remember when God moved in a mighty way in my own life.

Most of these stories that you have just read were about my just doing life and then recognizing that God was right there with me. Or maybe I have that backward, maybe it is actually realizing that God is life and yet I previously thought I was doing it on my own. I'm glad to know that the Lord is always there for us and has a way of opening our eyes to delightful adventures and surprises.

God is in our everyday life, and I also know when I am willing to step out in faith and do something that honors God then I have an opportunity to see the Almighty move in even more ways. I used to think that I had to wait for God to give me the official go-ahead to move forward on things, but it has occurred to me that God has already given us guidance in Scripture to be doing things that demonstrate love to others. And it is when I take that step to reach out to others in love that I end up seeing and experiencing even more of God.

With that in mind, in some of the stories included in this book I mentioned various organizations that are focused on sharing God's love in order to make this world a better place. The next few pages give more details about those organizations and provide contact information in case you would like to find out more or get involved. Your purchasing this book will help benefit each of these organizations mentioned, but my greatest hope is that you will take the time to get involved with some of them and really share and experience God's love.

God is moving in so many mighty ways around us. Let's not miss an opportunity to be a part of it. I hope this book has opened your eyes to some of the ways that you can be aware of God's presence. My greatest prayer for you is that you will recognize the divine presence of God all around you every single day! Amen and amen!

Supported Ministries and Charities

MY MAIN PURPOSE IN life is to share the good news of Jesus Christ; so, my time, my tithe, and my main focus is toward the body of Christ—the church. Yet I also recognize that there are some incredible godly organizations who are making a big difference in the lives of others and I want to make sure that I am supporting and encouraging them as well.

This book of God-stories mentions four of the ministries/charities in which I am involved. I wanted to let you know that the proceeds from the sale of this book will help support these organizations. I encourage you to check them out and find if there are ways that you can be involved to support their missions to make a difference in this world. Remember, you are blessed to be a blessing.[1] Share the talents and resources that God has given you and I know you will definitely see God moving in a mighty way.

From Divine Encounter 29—A Precious Gift

Children's Organ Transplant Association®

COTA is a national nonprofit organization dedicated to raising money for transplant-related expenses for children and young adults.

Website: www.cota.org

---

1. 2 Cor 9:11.

From Divine Encounter 39—From Killing Fields to New Life

Heart for Cambodia exists to spread the gospel of Jesus' love to the people of Cambodia. Many in Cambodia have never even heard of Jesus Christ. Through this ministry the message is being shared to change lives, and churches are being planted to transform communities.

Contact: Rev. Chiv In

Website: www.heartforcambodia.org

From Divine Encounters 40, 41, and 42

Baptizing in India, New Eyes to See God, and God Knows the Depth

Faith Hope and Charities Ministry is a nonprofit Christian ministry based in Dallas, Texas, USA, catering to the needs of village pastors and orphan children in Nellore, Andra Pradesh, South India. My Father's House Orphanage is under the umbrella of Faith Hope and Charity Ministries.

Contact: Luke and Kasthuri Raju

Website: www.faithhopeandcharityministries.org

From Divine Encounter 45—Faith Pointing

High Rise Day Habilitation Center is a loving place for adults with developmental and intellectual challenges. The various daily activities are chosen to encourage the development of skills and appropriate behavior, greater independence, community inclusion, relationship building, and self-advocacy. Costs for the center are beyond the small amount that comes from the state or a few of the parents. A special thanks to others who continually help to support this ministry.

Contact: Jeri Barnett and Jessica Pena

Website: www/highrisedayhab.org